Beowulf: A Translation

BEOWULF

A Translation

Thomas Meyer

punctum books ∗ brooklyn, ny

BEOWULF: A TRANSLATION
© Thomas Meyer, 2012.

First published in 2012 by
punctum books
Brooklyn, New York
punctumbooks.com

punctum books is an open-access and print-on-demand independent publisher dedicated to radically creative modes of intellectual inquiry and writing across a whimsical para-humanities assemblage. We specialize in neo-traditional and non-conventional scholarly work that productively twists and/or ignores academic norms, with an emphasis on books that fall length-wise between the article and the full-length book—id est, novellas in one sense or another. We also take in strays. This is a space for the imp-orphans of your thought and pen, an ale-serving church for little vagabonds.

ISBN-10: 0615612652
ISBN-13: 978-0615612652

Library of Congress Cataloging-in-Publication Data is available from the Library of Congress.

Front flyleaf drawing by Heather Masciandaro. The drawing on the frontispiece of *Part II: Homelands* is a plan of a large building at Hofsthahir, Iceland, most likely a farmhouse, although the element *hof-* suggests it may have once been a pagan temple.

for MJW
Anew
Again

TABLE OF CONTENTS

PREFACE:

AN EXPERIMENTAL POETIC ADVENTURE

David Hadbawnik

Last year, I had the opportunity to edit and publish a portion of poet Jack Spicer's *Beowulf* translation, undertaken many years ago during his graduate studies at Berkeley, and existing only in handwritten manuscript form in his archive in the Bancroft Library. As I prepared that edition for CUNY's Lost and Found Document Series,[1] working with general editor Ammiel Alcalay and my co-editor Sean Reynolds, my friend Richard Owens casually mentioned *another* unknown translation of this text by *another* avant-garde poet from the previous generation — this one, by Thomas Meyer. Owens, who had worked on the Jargon Society archive in the Poetry Collection at the University at Buffalo, had struck up a friendship with its founder, Jonathan Williams, and after Williams' death maintained a correspondence with his partner, Tom Meyer.

Meyer had been known to me as a criminally neglected poet of exceedingly fine abilities — such as his chapbook *Coromandel*, published by small but important independent press Skanky Possum in 2003. He had studied with Robert Kelly at Bard College and Gerrit Lansing was a friend at that same time, and he'd cut his

---

[1] See David Hadbawnik and Sean Reynolds, eds., *Jack Spicer's Beowulf, Parts I-II*, CUNY Poetics Documents Initiative, Series 2.5 (Spring 2011).

teeth in, and emerged from, that niche of poets who'd been impacted by the brief moment of vibrant cross-pollination between U.K. and U.S. experimental poetry in the late 1960s and early 1970s — a movement inspired by Ezra Pound, fueled by interactions among figures like Ed Dorn, J.H. Prynne, and Basil Bunting (see my interview with Meyer in Appendix A for more on his relationship with Bunting), and quickly overshadowed by the burgeoning Language Writing movement. In summary, it is this lineage, its concern with rigor, old forms, and translation, that explains both the existence of this translation and its decades-long neglect.

In short order, via Owens, I acquired a PDF copy of the text. Immediately it was clear that this was a translation in every sense of the word — taking liberties and risks with the Old English verse in astonishing ways. From a purely visual standpoint — as readers will quickly discover perusing the pages that follow — I had never seen anything quite like it. Certainly not in the numerous other translations of *Beowulf* that I'd studied and sampled, and really not of *any* poem, at least not in such a sustained and persistently experimental (yet persistently cohesive, and simply *fun*) manner. That includes Jack Spicer's *Beowulf*, which sadly, though it foreshadows his later translation experiments, and helps explain and contextualize his lifelong concern with the roots of language, does not reflect the kind of freedom and wildness of his "dictated" poetics beginning with *After Lorca*. Meyer's *Beowulf* provides the kind of experimental poetic adventure that the poem has long deserved.

The rest of the story partakes of a similar serendipity. Rich Owens, Micah Robbins (publisher of Interbirth Books), and I had talked about beginning a collaborative press, and I had hoped to approach Meyer about publishing his *Beowulf* on it. Meanwhile, preparing some remarks for the International Medieval Congress at Kalamazoo on Spicer's *Beowulf*, I included some images of Meyer's text in my presentation. Those images — with their visually arresting typographical arrangements and radical departures from standard form—stole the show, drawing enthusiastic responses from medievalists in the audience, including Eileen Joy and Jeffrey

Jerome Cohen, members of the BABEL Working Group[2] that had sponsored our panel. Encouraged by this, and the news about the new open-access publishing venture, punctum books, co-directed by BABEL members Eileen Joy and Nicola Masciandaro, it struck me that this might be a more appropriate venue for this text to finally emerge from the shadows. Returning to Buffalo, I pitched the idea to Tom Meyer and the editors of punctum, and the enthusiastic agreement of all confirmed this choice.

In a way, this publication is a token of faith. The tangled web of associations that led to my discovery of the translation, contact with Meyer, and bringing the text to punctum books, reveals an intersection of experimental poetics and academic (medieval) pursuits that doesn't happen nearly enough. Too often, there are strains and cliques of poetry, sealed off in advance from certain voices and tendencies. Likewise, there are worlds of academia and medieval studies that might look with suspicion on a nontraditional *Beowulf* such as this. Yet, as more and more contemporary poets — such as Daniel Remein, who provides the critical background to Meyer's *Beowulf* in the Introduction here — turn to medieval studies to follow the academic tracks of previous generations of avant-garde poets, such as the Berkeley Renaissance circle of Jack Spicer, Robin Blaser, and Robert Duncan, more connections such as this one will come to light, and further interactions and collaborations will become possible. Thus, we believe with the directors of punctum books that it's the perfect time for Tom Meyer's *Beowulf* — for those interested in experimental poetry, those eager to explore translations of medieval texts, and everyone in between.

---

[2] See the BABEL Working Group's website at http://www.babelworking group.org.

INTRODUCTION:

LOCATING *BEOWULF*

Daniel C. Remein

> Perhaps Wedermark, homeland of Beowulf and his
> dragon, can legitimately claim nothing but a dream status.
> Yet, in the secret fastness of my heart, I know I have been
> there.
> > Gillian Overing and Marijane Osborn

> There can be no duration (time of the poem) without
> *materium* — without the place where the strains are by
> which the enduring objects are made known.
> > Charles Olson

> There is not much poetry in the world like this . . . .
> > J.R.R. Tolkien

The Old English poem known in the modern era as *Beowulf* consists of some 3182 lines of alliterative verse. The poem is preserved on folios 129r to 198v of a unique and badly damaged Anglo-Saxon manuscript sometimes called the 'Nowell Codex' and now known by its shelf mark as the London, British Library, MS. Cotton Vitellius A.xv. The text was copied by two different scribes, bound alongside a poetic version of *Judith* (the deuterocanonical Biblical narrative), a prose version of the *Life of Saint Christopher*, and two texts of marvelous geography known as *The Wonders of the East* and *Alexander's Letter to Aristotle*. Dating the poem remains a point of scholarly controversy between the views of 'early' and 'late' daters: spanning from some time not too long after the Anglo-Saxon migration to Britain to a late ninth-century or even early eleventh-century (post-Viking invasion and settlement) Anglo-Danish political and cultural moment.[3] As R.M. Liuzza notes, "on strictly historical grounds, then, there is no period in Anglo-Saxon history in which a poem like *Beowulf* might not have been written or appreciated."[4] However, in terms of its textuality, the *Beowulf* we have is actually a very late Anglo-Saxon manuscript from the late tenth or even early eleventh century.[5]

Many students who read translations of the poem only under compulsion often rely on critical introductions that, as Allen Frantzen has explained, tend to offer a false sense of scholarly consensus about the poem and a historical frame delineated entirely in terms of a romanticized image of a Germanic antiquity (at least in part an invention of nineteenth-century criticism) that has long been critically dismantled.[6] Such a poem is often still imagined as the invention of inspired oral poets who sing only of heroic deeds,

---

[3] Cf. Colin Chase, ed., *The Dating of Beowulf* (1981; repr. Toronto: University of Toronto Press, 1997), and John D. Niles, "Locating *Beowulf* in Literary History," *Exemplaria* 5 (1993): 79-109, reprinted in *The Postmodern Beowulf*, eds. Eileen A. Joy and Mary K. Ramsey (Morgantown: West Virginia University Press, 2007), 131–162.

[4] R.M. Liuzza, "Introduction," in *Beowulf: A New Verse Translation*, trans. Roy M. Liuzza (Toronto: Broadview, 2000), 28.

[5] Niles, "Locating *Beowulf*," in *The Postmodern Beowulf*, 143. On the dating of the poem specifically in relation to its manuscript context, see also Kevin Kiernan, *Beowulf and the Beowulf Manuscript* (New Brunswick: Rutgers University Press, 1981).

[6] See Allen Frantzen, *Desire for Origins: New Language, Old English, and Teaching the Tradition* (New Brunswick: Rutgers University Press, 1990), esp. Chapter 6, "Writing the Unreadable *Beowulf*," reprinted in Joy and Ramsey, eds., *The Postmodern Beowulf*. See also E.G. Stanley, *The Search for Anglo-Saxon Paganism* (Cambridge: Cambridge University Press, 1975), 91-130.

monsters, and loyalty. As a result, *Beowulf* is a poem that many may think we know pretty well, a poem from which we should not expect much new or surprising. However, since the time of the first modern critical attempts to read the poem, critical understanding of *Beowulf* has undergone a series of radical shifts and transformations whose strange and often deeply embarrassing layers may leave the poem at once closer to hand and more unfamiliar than ever. As an encounter of *Beowulf* and twentieth-century avant-garde poetics, Thomas Meyer's translation of the poem can be understood as another transformation of this critical history.

THE UNKNOWABLE *BEOWULF*: THE CRITICS AND THE POETS

Other than the speculation that the *Beowulf*-manuscript likely passed from monastic into private ownership following the dissolution of the monasteries in England by Henry VIII, more or less nothing is known of what happened to it until the collector Lawrence Nowell inscribed his name on the first leaf in 1563.[7] The manuscript was later acquired by Sir Robert Cotton (1571-1631) and was damaged in the Cotton Library fire in 1731. The first known critical comment on *Beowulf* in print did not appear until Sharon Turner's second edition of his *History of the Anglo-Saxons* (1805).[8] A copyist working for the Icelandic scholar Grímur Thorkelin more famously transcribed the poem in 1787, and later Thorkelin himself made a copy.[9] Thorkelin's own early print edition of the

---

[7] See *Klaeber's Beowulf and the Fight at Finnsburg*, 4th edn., eds. R.D. Fulk, Robert E. Bjork, and John D. Niles (Toronto: University of Toronto Press, 2008), xxvi. Critic Kevin Kiernan has speculated that Queen Elizabeth's' Lord Treasurer William Cecil may have passed the book to Nowell, and that one John Bale (d. 1563) may have had the book earlier on. See Kevin Kiernan, *Beowulf and the Beowulf MS*, rev. edn. (Ann Arbor: University of Michigan Press, 1996).

[8] See Daniel G. Calder, "The Study of Style in Old English Poetry: A Historical Introduction," in *Old English Poetry: Essays on Style*, ed. Daniel G. Calder (Berkeley: University of California Press, 1979), 8.

[9] Because of the damage to the manuscript by the Cotton Library fire, these transcripts remain invaluable to editorial work on the poem,

poem (along with a Latin translation) is full of guesswork, and so John Mitchell Kemble's 1833 edition presented the first complete modern scholarly edition of the poem. Following Kemble, and alongside a flurry of publications on the poem, a number of editions appeared (many by German scholars), including that of Danish scholar N.F.S. Grundtvig in 1861. Frederick Klaeber's 1922 *Beowulf and the Fight at Finnsburgh*, the standard scholarly edition of the poem, was completely revised by R.D. Fulk, Robert E. Bjork, and John D. Niles for a fourth edition in 2008.

John Josias Conybeare, one of the first scholars to begin to understand Anglo-Saxon alliteration and its metrical importance, offered English translations of long passages of the poem in his *Illustrations of Anglo-Saxon Poetry* in 1826. Kemble published the first full-length English translation in 1837. Relatively recent translations of more immediate interest to the reader of this volume might include Michael Alexander's, which remains the text of the Penguin Classics edition of the poem (1973); R.M. Liuzza's translation and introduction (1999); and Seamus Heaney's bestselling translation, which was commissioned by the *Norton Anthology of English Literature* (2000).

The earliest critical views of the poem often involve a dismissal of the poem as "barbaric" or lacking any prosodical structure. Strangely, this view developed alongside competing claims on the poem as national epic (which would eventually support and receive motivation from Nazi and other racist historical narratives of an idealized Germanic past).[10] By the early twentieth century, the work of Frederick Klaeber and W.P. Ker consolidated the major critical

---

although, ironically, Thorkelin's own copy is often thought to be the less accurate.

[10] See Frantzen, *Desire for Origins*, 62–74; Liuzza, "Introduction," in *Beowulf: A New Verse Translation*, 12; and Calder, "The Study of Style in Old English Poetry," in *Old English Poetry: Essays on Style*, esp. 1–29. On this history of philology, including its nationalist dimensions, see Haruko Momma, *From Philology to English Studies: Language and Culture in the Nineteenth Century* (forthcoming from Cambridge University Press) and also Momma's forthcoming essay in *Communicative Spaces: Variation, Contact, and Change*, eds. Claudia Lange, Beatrix Weber, and Göran Wolf.

orientation around an interest in the poem's capacity to help the historian shed light on Germanic antiquity. Klaeber in particular regretted that the material in the poem that he thought could "disclose a magnificent historic background" played little role, while the narrative with which the poem is concerned consists of an "inferior" story preoccupied with monsters and the marvelous.[11] All these shifts are dwarfed by the effect of J.R.R. Tolkien's 1936 lecture "*Beowulf*: The Monsters and the Critics," which argued that the poem should not stand or fall in its critical appraisal as a classical epic or a more or less adequate representation of a certain Germanic past (arguing in particular for the centrality of the "fabulous" monster elements in the poem). Tolkien's lecture could be considered in hindsight to have at once "saved" the poem for New Criticism and to have reduced the critical approaches to the poem to a choice between history and aesthetics.

However, any summary judgment of Tolkien's influence in the critical history of *Beowulf* may be unfair. In making *Beowulf* available to critical readings informed by the New Criticism (with all of its serious attendant problems), Tolkien also made possible certain strong attempts to think about the poem's poetics — through which *Beowulf* criticism impinged directly on avant-garde poetry.[12] Arthur Brodeur, and later, Stanley B. Greenfield, offered

---

[11] See Fr. Klaeber, "Introduction," in Fr. Klaeber, ed., *Beowulf and the Fight at Finnsburgh*, 3rd edn. (Boston: D.C. Heath, 1950), liv–lv.

[12] See J.R.R. Tolkien, "Beowulf: the Monsters and the Critics," *Proceedings of the British Academy*, Vol. 22 (1936; repr. Oxford: Oxford University Press, 1952). The situation of Europe in 1936 when Tolkien gave his lecture is not unimportant to his final conclusion that the poem "would still have power had it been written in some time or place unknown and without posterity, if it contained no name that could now be recognized or identified by research. Yet it is in fact written in a language that after many centuries has still essential kinship with out own, it was made in this land, and moves in our northern world beneath our northern sky, and for those who are native to that tongue and land, it must ever call with a profound appeal — until the dragon comes" (36). While Tolkien's allusions to modern English and modern England in particular are not without their own nationalist ring, the poem is here framed as worthy of aesthetic study not in order to cut it off forever from consideration of how it relates to

aesthetic readings which insisted on the ability of modern criticism to discuss the literary merits of Old English verse (against the assertions of proponents of Oral-formulaic theory such as Francis P. Magoun).[13] Brodeur's *Beowulf* course at Berkeley — wherein he insisted that the poem can be read and experienced as, can stand or fall alongside, a modern poem — played an important role in the development of the poetics and the friendship of Berkeley Renaissance poets Jack Spicer and Robin Blaser.[14] The importance of *Beowulf* to the circle of Spicer, Blaser, and Robert Duncan is currently emerging from relative critical obscurity thanks to David Hadbawnik and Sean Reynold's recent edition of Spicer's *Beowulf*.[15] Meyer's translation again reminds us that the importance of *Beowulf* to poets writing in the American avant-garde remains a significant strain of the poem's critical history. A truncated list of the sites of its importance in the early and later twentieth century would include Ezra Pound's shorter poetry and the *Cantos,* W.H. Auden's early work,[16] Basil Bunting's long poem *Briggflatts* (1966), and

---

history, but to de-legitimate the search for *Beowulf*'s relations to history which could be pressed into the service of Nazi ideology. The way the poem is going to move under *our* northern sky is going to be categorically different than the way it moves in service of a narrative of fascism.

[13] See Arthur G. Brodeur, *The Art of Beowulf* (Berkeley: University of California Press, 1959), esp. 69–70; Stanley G. Greenfield, *The Interpretation of Old English Poems* (London: Routledge, 1972); and Stanley G. Greenfield, trans., *A Readable Beowulf: The Old English Epic Newly Translated* (Carbondale: Southern Illinois University Press, 1982).

[14] See David Hadbawnik, "'*Beowulf* Is A Hoax': Jack Spicer's Medievalism," in David Hadbawnik and Sean Reynolds, eds., *Jack Spicer's Beowulf*, Part 1, CUNY Poetics Documents Initiative, Series 2.5 (Spring 2011): 2–3.

[15] This is the result of careful work by David Hadbawnik and Sean Reynolds: see their *Jack Spicer's Beowulf*, noted above.

[16] See Daniel C. Remein, "Auden, Translation, Betrayal: Radical Poetics and Translation from Old English," *Literature Compass* 8.11 (Nov. 2011): 811–29. Many look to Pound's *Seafarer* and *Canto 1* as a navigational point. It was Auden, however, who suggested, for all of Pound's attention to meter, his technical failure: "Pound forgot not to alliterate on the last lift, Anglo-Saxon doesn't do that." See the Robert H. Boyer Interview of Neville

Michael Alexander's translations, which attracted the attention of, among others, Robert Creeley.[17]

A largely historicist and patristic orientation followed the New Critical readings of the poem, and when "theory" finally hit *Beowulf* full force in the 1990s, criticism again underwent a transformation. In 1990 Gillian Overing published her feminist critique of the poem's signifying system.[18] And by the decade's close, Jeffrey Jerome Cohen's *Of Giants: Sex, Monsters, and the Middle Ages* re-oriented *Beowulf* studies by pairing a reading of the monsters of the poem in terms of Lacanian and Kristevan semiotics with a deep concern for the poem's affective work.[19] In the wake of the theory-driven readings of the poem from the 1990s, Eileen A. Joy and Mary K. Ramsey's collection *The Postmodern Beowulf* further reconfigured the place of the poem by drawing attention to the way that *Beowulf* criticism had already engaged in theory and how easily the poem fit into that discourse, and also by insisting on the pertinence of *Beowulf* to particularly postmodern experiences of gender, loss, identity, and historical memory.

At the beginning of these last ("postmodern") shifts in how we think and read *Beowulf*, critic Allen Franzten admitted that "*Beowulf* is an incomplete text, incompletely attested, and it will always be

---

Coghill and W.H. Auden (Columbia University Libraries, Special Collections, H. Carpenter Papers).

[17] Creeley's 1972 *A Day Book* opens with an epigraph from Alexander's translation OE Riddle 29: "To build itself a hideaway high up in the city,/ a room in a tower, timbered with art,/ was all it aimed at, if only it might," see Michael Alexander, *The Earliest English Poems* (New York: Penguin, 2008), 73.

[18] Gillian R. Overing, *Language, Sign, and Gender in Beowulf* (Carbondale: Southern Illinois University Press, 1990).

[19] Jeffrey Jerome Cohen, *Of Giants: Sex, Monsters, and the Middle Ages* (Minneapolis: University of Minnesota Press, 1999). See Chapter 1, "The Ruins of Identity," 1–28. Cohen's work appeared contemporaneously to Andy Orchard's study of the entire *Beowulf* manuscript as a book about monsters. See Andy Orchard, *Pride and Prodigies: Studies in the Monsters of the Beowulf-Manuscript* (Cambridge: D.S. Brewer, 1995).

controversial."[20] James W. Earl offered this confession in his 1994 landmark study *Thinking About 'Beowulf'*:

> I no longer trust those who say they know what *Beowulf* means, or what it is about. The poem is hedged about with so many uncertainties — historical, textual, linguistic, hermeneutic — that even the simplest and most straightforward statements can provoke a battle royal among scholars.[21]

This critical history testifies to the extent that *Beowulf* is a poem we do not understand, and, over two decades after the postmodern turns in the poem's critical history began, *Beowulf* criticism is perhaps primed once again for another shock.

LOCATING MEYER'S *BEOWULF*

Simply put, Meyer's translation demonstrates that radical twentieth-century poetics harbor practices of making relations to *Beowulf* in new and necessary ways. As an alternative to the representational, Meyer's *Beowulf* makes possible relations to the poem in terms of *locating* and then topographically exploring the poem. When I asked Meyer about the question of place in his translation, he explained, "Living in the north of England and in contact with [Basil] Bunting, the 'North' was certainly a powerful presence. Yet in my *Beowulf*, it was 'here' and 'there.' 'Now' and 'then.'"[22] Translating the poem in the West Riding of Yorkshire, near Northumbria — the site of political and ecclesiastical hegemony in the Age of Bede — results in the insight that *Beowulf*'s poetics seem fundamentally preoccupied with crossing elementary terms of worldly topographical and historical perception *as such* (here/there, now/then). The translation thus collects together the various ways twentieth-century long poems approach histories lodged within a

---

[20] Frantzen, *Desire for Origins*, 171.
[21] James W. Earl, *Thinking About Beowulf* (Stanford: Stanford University Press, 1994), 11.
[22] Thomas Meyer, private correspondence, 25 September, 2011.

place while giving rise to the poem in turn as its own "place," paying particular attention to the visual qualities of these poetics. Discussing the range of its formal strategies, Meyer explains, "[T]he project wound up being a kind of typological specimen book for long American poems extant circa 1965. Having variously the 'look' of Pound's *Cantos*, Williams' *Paterson*, or Olson or Zukofsky, occasionally late Eliot, even David Jones."[23]

Perhaps most saliently, the topographical concerns of Charles Olson's Projective Verse (or Field Poetics) are played out at the level of typography. More broadly, the division of Meyer's translation into *Oversea* and *Homelands* aptly organizes the poem around the two main places around which the text of poem aggregates, and in turn invites readers to interface with the two sections topographically (*Oversea*: the land of Heorot and Hrothgar, Grendel, Grendel's mother, and the murky waters of her lake, et alia; *Homelands*: Wedermark, Hygelac, Beowulf's eventual kingship, and of course the dragon).

Turning to the topographical poetics of the poem brings to the fore a sense that is currently only quietly operative in *Beowulf* criticism. Klaeber influentially doubted whether "we can be sure that the Anglo-Saxon poet had a clear knowledge of Northern geography," and maintained that "the topographical hints contained in the poem could not be used successfully for definite localization."[24] More recently, James Earl has reasoned otherwise, insisting that "*we cannot assume the poem is representative of any period, or even, finally, representative of anything at all*," or, alternately, "*Beowulf* bore a complex, indirect, and nonmimetic relation to any historical reality"[25] — a logic implying not that the poem produces no site-specific relations, but that it traffics instead in non-representational ones. After all, there are some obvious "real" sites to which the poem can relate. John D. Niles argues that archaeological digs at Gamel Lejre in Zealand, Denmark, in 1986-1988 and 2001-2004, offer "hard evidence that the *Beowulf* poet's narrative, however fanciful it may be, is indeed grounded in that

---

[23] Quoted in David Hadbawnik, private correspondence [n.d.].
[24] Klaeber, "Introduction," in *Beowulf and the Fight at Finnsburg*, xlvii.
[25] Earl, *Thinking About Beowulf*, 17, 167.

locale."[26] Scholars Gillian Overing and Marijane Osborn, relying on a hired and enthusiastic boat captain, old maps, and *Beowulf* itself, "attempted to literally 'reinvent' Beowulf's voyage to Heorot" (sailing to Lejre, Denmark) and by implication plausibly locate Wedermark and the homeland of the Geats.[27] Along with C.L. Wrenn, Overing and Osborn locate Wedermark as the home of the historical *gautar* in modern-day Götland, Sweden, where they begin their reinvention of Beowulf's voyage.[28] They conclude that "the *Beowulf* poet . . . knew in some measure of the visual reality of which he wrote," and Osborn implies a possible affinity of parts of the poem itself to an iron-age-style oral map for landmark sea-navigation.[29] The two scholars demonstrate that *Beowulf* has the remarkable capacity to physically move people through actual places on earth, which suggests a particularly non-representational relation of the poem to place: a poetic cartography less of representational maps than the sort of Anglo-Saxon linguistic map studied by the late critic Nicholas Howe (exemplified by Anglo-Saxon legal boundary-clauses) — less a representation of, than a procedural interface with, the landscape.[30]

---

[26] John D. Niles, "Introduction," in *Beowulf and Lejre*, ed. John D. Niles (Tempe: Arizona Center of Medieval and Renaissance Studies, 2007), 1. On the idea that the archaeology behind the poem can only ever be wishful and/or phantasmic, see also Helen T. Bennet, "The Postmodern Hall in *Beowulf*: Endings Embedded in Beginnings," *The Heroic Age* 12 (2009): http://www.heroicage.org/issues/12/ba.php, and Roberta Frank, "*Beowulf* and Sutton Hoo: The Odd Couple," in *The Archaeology of Anglo-Saxon England: Basic Readings*, ed. Catherine Karkov (New York: Garland Publishing Company, 1999), 317–38.

[27] Gillian Overing and Marijane Osborn, *Landscape of Desire: Partial Stories of the Medieval Scandinavian World* (Minneapolis: University of Minnesota Press, 1994), 1.

[28] Overing and Osborn, *Landscape of Desire*, 1. See, generally, xii–37.

[29] Overing and Osborn, *Landscape of Desire*, xv, 17.

[30] See Overing and Osborn, *Landscape of Desire,* 12, 16–17, and Nicholas Howe, *Writing the Map of Anglo-Saxon England: Essays in Cultural Geography* (New Haven: Yale University Press, 2008), 29–46.

Meyer's translation of Beowulf's sea-crossing to Heorot (Klaeber's lines 205–24b)[31] makes for a nice specimen of *Beowulf*'s commensurability with such a topographical poetics:

15 sought seawood,
led to land's edge
by seawise warrior,

set keel to breakers,

left
    shore's ledge,
leapt
    churned sand.

Sea surge bore forth
    bright cargo:

weapons, trappings,
hearts keen to man
    timberbound,
wavelapped,
    windwhipped,
foamthroated bird.

Ship floated. Sail filled.
A day & a day prow plowed
& crew saw bright cliffs,
steep hills, wide beaches.

Sea crossed. Land at last.
Boat moored. Byrnes shook.

---

[31] All citations of the Old English text of *Beowulf* from *Klaeber's Beowulf and the Fight at Finnsburg*, 4th edn. Quotations unchanged except for the omission of diacritical marks.

It is not difficult to see how the poem literalizes the crossing of the sea in the concrete space between these two columns of text, the first waving in its indents and the second a solid block.

Yet, the above lines do not operate most programmatically as a specimen of mere mimetic typography. The shift of the left justification of stanza across the page also recalls any number of moments from Olson's *Maximus* poems.[32] And the poetics of Olson's "Projective Verse" or "Field Composition" can helpfully frame this passage of Meyer's translation. Miriam Nichols has recently discussed the site-specific poetics of Projective Verse in terms of relations of "cosmicity" which remain particularly viable in our moment of ecological disaster.[33] As it pertains to Meyer's translation and to *Beowulf*, Olson explains that Projective Verse conceives of poiesis as a radically open form in which "FORM IS NEVER MORE THAN AN EXTENSION OF CONTENT" and also in which, for the poet, "From the moment he ventures into FIELD COMPOSITION — puts himself in the open — he can go by no track other than the one the poem under hand declares, for itself."[34] Olson writes: "A poem is energy transferred from where the poet got it (he will have some several causations), by way of the poem itself to, all the way over to, the reader. Okay. Then the poem itself must, at all points, be a high-energy construct and, at all points, an energy-discharge."[35] This sense of transfers of/from multiple points of energy that nonetheless holds together as a "Field" leaves us with a sense of the poem as itself an emergent site with finite but intense points of contiguity with the places of its energy transfers — a site made in projectively *contiguous* (topographical, *not* representational) relation

---

[32] Charles Olson, *The Maximus Poems*, ed. George F. Butterick (Berkeley: University of California Press, 1983), cf. 32, 35, 150–156 ('Letter May 2, 1959'), 299, 441–45.

[33] See Miriam Nichols, "Charles Olson: Architect of Place," in *Radical Affections: Essays on the Poetics of Outside* (Tuscaloosa: University of Alabama Press, 2010), 18–64.

[34] Charles Olson, "Projective Verse," in *Collected Prose*, eds. Donald Allen and Benjamin Friedlander (Berkeley: University of California Press, 1997), 240.

[35] Olson, "Projective Verse," 240.

to specific worldly sites (although authenticated less in terms of its worldly sites than the worldly quality of its procedures and particular field). Projective Verse frames the poem itself as a worldly place that can in turn move the reader though the physical world (Olson's *Maximus*, for instance, includes examples of mimetic carto-typography such as a map of the Gloucester harbor produced by typewriter characters arranged on the page by orienting it at various angles in the typewriter).[36] In some of Olson's recently published notes, he more exactingly frames how the poem's non-representational paths (its form as extension of content) result in aggregating in turn another literal site:

> A poem is a 'line' between any two points in creation . . . . In its passage it includes—in the meaning here it passes through—the material of itself. Such material is the 'field' . . . . This is only possibly if both line and field stay weighted with the individual peculiarities of the poem's relevant environment—its idiosyncratic quality of being itself, of being 'obstructive' at the same time that it is lucid, and of immediate worth.[37]

The above-cited translation of the sea-voyage by Meyer, with its movement from one side of the page to the other, proceeds by exactly such a passage of the poem though the material of itself as a topographical field. Meyer twists the narration of the Old English into a tight knot. The Old English reads:

> guman ut scufon,
> weras on wilsiþ   wudu bundenne.
> Gewat þa ofer wægholm   winde gefysed
> flota famiheals   fugle gelicost,
> oð þæt ymb antid oþres dogores
> wundenstefna   gewaden hæfde

---

[36] See Charles Olson, *The Maximus Poems*, 156; see another such map on 150.

[37] Charles Olson, *The Principle of Measure in Composition by Field: Projective Verse II*, ed. Joshua Hoeynck (Tuscon: Chax Press, 2010), 15.

þæt ða liþende land gesawon (ll. 215b–21)

And R.M. Liuzza's translation which closely maps the OE syntax offers:

> . . . the men pushed off
> on their wished-for journey in that wooden vessel.
> Over the billowing waves, urged by the wind,
> the foamy-necked floater flew like a bird,
> until due time on the second day
> the curved-prowed vessel had come so far
> that the seafarers sighted land (ll. 215–21)

In Meyer's translation the staggered lines of this narration typographically grapple with the appositive style of Old English verse. The indentations of the entire first column of text overlap with ceasura-like line breaks to both visually and audibly place the phrases "shore's edge" and "churned sand" into the topographical crevices of the field of the poem held by the energy-field of the alliterating verbs "left" and "leapt." The waving block of text forms a single shining summit of all the items that constitute the "bright cargo" and so gives place to the perception of the ship as a "foamthroated bird." Meyer thus works and twists the surface of the Old English poem into a knotted and wound-up topography — making it lucidly felt how *Beowulf* can move a person between these points of high-energy transfer along a line from Götland to Lejre. In this way the site-specificity of *Beowulf* is related to its specific internal self-organization, the "idiosyncratic quality of being itself," which gives rise to the poem's "obstructive" quality, its specific ecosystem. This specific typographical arrangement materially obstructs the reader's passage through the poem and so opens onto a concrete ecology for *Beowulf* in modern English, onto the possibility of a nonrepresentational relation to cliffs literary and geographical, a place where the sea-cliffs of the poem can take place in the present.

Meyer's *Beowulf*, however, is not trying to send us back to an authentic transcendent place that would secure the authority of either translation or Anglo-Saxon poem — although, as poet and critic Lytle Shaw notes, it is the tendency of mid-twentieth-century poetics to slip into exactly this trap.[38] As an alternative to the traps of using the term "place" (and its art-history counterpart "site-specificity") in an attempt to exhaustively ground and authenticate a given work, Shaw examines how rhetorical framing in certain contemporary poetics gives rise to discursive "sites" that are best treated literally as sites in which the very frame of site-specificity functions "less as an authoritative interpretive model that gives traction to a docent's account of a particular location than as a discursive site that must *itself* be explored archaeologically." In other words, the synchronic framing of site specificity itself requires diachronic framing of the pasts and futures of its rhetoric.[39]

This is of course the very effect of Meyer's pastiche of modernist long-poem forms: a translation that doubles as a museum of exhibits of modernist experiment requiring its own docent. Thus in the above-cited translation of the voyage to Heorot, Meyer quotes verbatim Ezra Pound's line "set keel to breakers." The line is taken from the opening of the very first of Pound's *Cantos*, which recasts the narrative of Odysseus' departure from Circe's island in a verse reminiscent of Anglo-Saxon meter. Meyer's translation invites an archaeological or geological investigation of its topography, from which uncoils a whole other set of literary histories that inescapably inhere in *Beowulf* in the present.

TRANSLATING DETAILS

An instance of what at first may seem more conventional typo-graphy in Meyer's translation — Hrothgar's description of the path to the lake of Grendel's mother — instead witnesses the capacity for *Beowulf* (in Old English and its translation) to appear in terms of an attention to concrete elements on the minutest and subtlest of levels:

---

[38] See Lytle Shaw, "Docents of Discourse," *boundary 2* 36.3 (2009): 25–47.
[39] Shaw, "Docents of Discourse," 47.

. . . I'm told two *things*
can be seen to prowl the nearby
borderlands, a male & female,
who dwell in swamps on

[*page break*]

"dark land

riddled with
wolfhills, windy

cliffs, risky
swamptrails where

upland streams

glimpsed
through cragfog

flow on underground.

Not far,
a few miles from here,

a firmly rooted wood's
frost crusted branches

hand
shadows upon a lake

where each night sees
strange wonders:

firewaters,

flare above

unplumbed fathoms."

Here, the short lines of the couplets and single lines do appear as the list of landmarks in a textual map, or, in modern terms, a set of directions (the capacity for *Beowulf* to provide textual maps translated into driving directions). In doing so, the concrete lines construct a slim column of text around which the passage to the lake and the lake itself coagulate together as a site charged with the energy of vertical movement — the lines connecting fire and water and atmosphere form exactly the single frightening mass the Old English poem offers. But while this passage lends itself to the terms of Projective Verse in making manifest the poem's latent capacity to appear as modern, it also expands the translation's range of reference to twentieth-century poetics.

In particular, the ability of this column of text to stand on its own by manner of the slow and exact allowances of detail across these short lines also displays Meyer's *Beowulf* taking shape in terms of Louis Zukofsky's articulation of "Objectivist" poetics. Compare Meyer's passage to this early passage from Zukosfky's "A":

> Giant sparkler,
> Lights of the river,
>
> (Horses turning)
> Tide,
>
> And pier lights
> Under a light of the hill,
>
> A lamp on the leaf-green
> Lampost seen by the light
>
> Of a trick (a song)
> Lanterns swing behind horses,
>
> Their sides gleam

From levels of water —[40]

The work of the loose group of poets included under the rubric of Objectivist writing (including Rezinikov, Oppen, Niedecker, and Rakosi — modernist, running from the early 1930s and into the 1970s) follows a trajectory that both overlaps and significantly diverges from the tendencies and timeline of Projective Verse and its loose group of practitioners (often hailed as early postmodern poetry, running from the very late 1940s into the 1980s). As Peter Nicholls explains, Objectivist verse comprises one of the ways that "American modernism . . . generated counter-movements *within itself*, movements which revised and contested what had gone before."[41] Objectivist verse is marked by a desire for exteriority.[42] For, the moniker for this "Objectivist" poetics is misleading, as it is not a poetry interested in concrete description of pre-existing objects the poet can take for granted, but the production of the poem as its own entity with its own reality of minute but exacting details. As Zukofsky explains, "writing occurs which is the detail, not mirage, of seeing"; not in order to represent an already extant object, but because "distinct from print which records action and existence and incites the mind to further suggestion, there exists, tho it may not be harbored as solidity in the crook of an elbow, writing . . . which is an object or affects the mind as such."[43] Moments of "sincerity," which Zukofsky's 1931 statement in *Poetry* (that became the de-facto manifesto for the poets about to be called the Objectivists) defines as the "accuracy of detail," form the basic units of a new objectified shape.[44] As Nicholls notes, for Objectivist

---

[40] Louis Zukofsky, *A-4*, in *"A"* (New York: New Directions, 2011), 12.

[41] Peter Nicholls, "Modernising Modernism: From Pound to Oppen," *Critical Quarterly* 44.2 (2002): 43.

[42] Nicholls, "Modernising modernism," 42.

[43] Louis Zukofsky, "Sincerity and Objectification, With Special Reference to the Work of Charles Reznikoff," *Poetry* 37.5 (1931): 273–74.

[44] Zukofsky, "Sincerity and Objectification," 273–74.

poets "what was objectified was the poem itself,"[45] just as Zukofsky explains objectification as a "rested totality," or "the apprehension satisfied completely as the appearance of the art form as an object."[46] Most broadly and schematically put, it is around the interest in the particular that Objectivist writing and Projective Verse converge, but around this sense of the poem as rested (in contrast to the kinetics of Field Composition), that the tension between the pull of Projective Verse and the pull of Objectivist writing can be felt in Meyer's translation.

Note how, in the quotation above, Meyer allows the phrase "upland streams" to sit as a self-sufficient unit of one-line stanza before it has to take its place within a subject noun-phrase of the couplet "upland streams // glimpsed / through cragfog," and then allows that phrase to rest before taking its place as the subject of a whole sentence: "upland streams // glimpsed / through cragfog // flow on underground." Each of these exacting units, with its attention to particularity, exemplifies precisely the "sincerity" that is to aggregate into the poem which rests in itself — and not without echoing Olson's sense of the specific idiosyncrasy of the poem.[47] Consider, for example, the translation of "risky / swamp-trails" for the Old English "frecne fengelad" (Liuzza gives us "awful fenpaths," l. 1359). The Old English adjective *frecne* most prominently means 'perilous' or 'dangerous,' but also appears in some instances with a moral inflection of wickedness or trickery (i.e., the danger resulting from wicked trickery found on the way to a monster's lake) and can thus give way to a translation marked by a cloudy uncertainty or a proliferation of terms. Instead, "risky / swamptrails" focuses these senses into a very particular, and frighteningly casual, specificity.

While this strange particularity and tangibility of the Objectivist poem does not seem generally incommensurate with

---

[45] Peter Nicholls, "Of Being Ethical: Reflections on George Oppen," in *The Objectivist Nexus*, eds. Rachel Blau DuPlessis and Peter Quartermain (Tuscaloosa: University of Alabama Press, 1999), 241.

[46] Zukofsky, "Sincerity and Objectification," 274.

[47] Zukofsky, "Sincerity and Objectification," 280; Olson, *Projective Verse II*, 15.

Field Composition, the Objectivist insistence on the *rested* exteriority of the poem-as-object would seem divergent from the contiguity of poem and world in Projectivist kinetics. The Objectivist poet follows, as Nicholls finds in George Oppen's work, "a desire for some pure exteriority which allows the 'ego' to be defined only at the point at which it runs up against what is not itself."[48] While similar to the obstructive quality of Olson's field, such an alterity would seem to produce less proximity to and less permeable boundaries with the kinds of place implicated in an energy-transfer from sources to readers. Accordingly, more Objectivist moments of Meyer's translation — such as the above passage of Hrothgar's description of the path to the Grendelkin lake — do feel different, and readers familiar with the Old English might detect a sense of (medieval) place to a lesser extent than in more Projective passages. This may be the result of a kind of omission less conventional in *Beowulf*-translation, a type of condensation that registers in terms offered by Lorine Niedecker (that poet only on the margins of the Objectivist group), who posited the poet's workspace as a 'condensery.'[49] Compare, for example, Meyer's above-cited rendition of the path to the lake of the Grendelkin to Klaeber's text, Liuzza's translation, as well as that of Edwin Morgan's 1952 text (a translation contemporary to Olson and Zukofsky that is at least mildly self-reflexive about its poetics and its "modernity"):[50]

> Hie dygel lond
> warigeað, wulfhleoþu,   windige næssas,
> frecne fengelad,   ðær fyrgenstream
> under næssa genipu   niþer gewiteð,
> flod under foldan.   Nis þæt feor heonon

---

[48] Nicholls, "Modernising modernism," 53.

[49] See Lorine Niedecker, "Poet's Work," in Lorine Niedecker *Collected Works*, ed. Jenny Penberthy (Berkeley: University of California Press, 2002), 194: "No layoff/ from this/ condensery."

[50] Edwin Morgan, *Beowulf: A Verse Translation Into Modern English* (Berkeley: University of California Press, 1952). Morgan's introduction patiently considers exactly how to construct the prosody of his translation in terms of an array of conservative and more adventurous modernisms.

milgemearces   þæt se mere standeð;
ofer þæm hongiað   hrinde bearwas,
 wudu wyrtum fæst   wæter oferhelmað.
þær mæg nihta gehwæm   niðwundor seon,
fyr on flode. No þæs frod leofað
gumena bearna,   þæt þone grund wite . . . .
(Klaeber, ll. 1357b–67).

. . . That murky land
they hold, wolf-haunted slopes, windy headlands,
awful fenpaths, where the upland torrents
plunge downward under the dark crags,
the flood underground. It is not far hence
—measured in miles—that the mere stands;
over it hangs a grove hoar-frosted,
a firm-rooted wood looming over the water.
Every night one can see there an awesome wonder,
fire on the water. There lives none so wise
or bold that he can fathom its abyss.
(Liuzza, 1357b–67)

. . . They guard a region
Uncouth, wolves' dunes, blustering headlands,
Desperate fen-ground, where the mountain-torrent
Falls down under the louring bluffs,
Pours down to earth. It is not far distant
Measured by miles that the lake lies;
A great-rooted wood throws shade on its water.
There a strange horror at night may be seen.
A blaze on the stream. Of the children of men
No one has wisdom that could plumb that abyss.
(Morgan1357b–67)

Meyer's translation does not register the flow and eddy of the variation as it is scattered through the passage in the Old English text — to which Liuzza and Morgan both faithfully attend. Meyer however expands the phrase *fyr on flode* [literally, "fire on the waters"] in a manner that also condenses the Old English. While the Old English does not produce variation specifically around this alliterative doublet, Meyer's translation first combines the three words *fyr on flode* into one ["firewaters"] and then expands it into a variation which incorporates the lines that follow in Old English: "firewaters, / flare above unplumbed depths." The lines condense the explanation that follows in the Old English (preserved by both Liuzza and Morgan) that none alive can perceive or understand the depths of the lake ["No þæs frod leofað / gumena bearna, þæt þone grund wite"] by distilling the two-line Old English explanation into the attribution of the adjective "unplumbed" to the noun "depths" (in this instance also a respectable translation of Old English *grund*). In tension with the vertical kinetics of this passage, Meyer incorporates the quality of being unfathomable into the exactness of a single detail, and thus leaves the unit more precise and more at rest within the arrangement of the passage. This condensation radicalizes the non-human alterity of the lake by removing the mitigating term of a perplexed human from its construction. In this way, Meyer's translation tends to avoid moments that purely exemplify a single distinct strain of twentieth-century poetics, producing instead an heroic attempt to balance Projectivist and Objectivist demands.

Paleography of the *Beowulf*-Typescript

The second section of the translation, *Homelands*, unfolds increasingly in small bits of print, demanding more page turns and granting more paper to each mark. Writing of his basic approach to the poem, Meyer explains, "instead of the text's orality, perhaps perversely I went for the visual. Deciding to use page layout (recto/verso) as a unit."[51] The groupings of only a few lines extend the apparent style of Poundian Imagism, the sincerities of Objective verse, and the Field of the Projective, by more carefully tending to the concrete page. At the moment of the encounter of the poem's famous dragon with the footprints of the slave responsible for the

---

[51] Thomas Meyer, interview with David Hadbawnik (in this volume).

theft of a cup from the dragon's hoard, Meyer gives an entire page to merely two words and a comma:

> manstink,
>> footprints

Perhaps, more than the vocabulary of active and germinal fecundity with which Pound described his earlier Imagism and Vorticism, this page recalls the economy of Pound's later use of the Chinese character that he understood to mean rest/hitching-post [*chih³*] as epitomizing a self-sufficient rest,[52] or the pages from Olson's *Maximus* with lone phrases on them such as "Veda upanishad edda than."[53] The visual impression of the print word "footprints" is here given enough concrete space to provoke the sensation of the non-visual "manstink" out from the hollow of a largely empty page. Meyer's translation drastically condenses the Old English text, which explains with a more conventional narrative sentence that "stearcheort onfand / feondes fotlast" [Liuzza: "stark-hearted he found/ his enemy's footprint," ll. 2288–89]. But by foregrounding the materiality of the word "footsteps" as print on a largely empty page, Meyer also renders concrete a latent sense of the Old English noun *fotlast,* the semantic content of which, as a compound of *fot* ['foot'] and the suffix *–last* ['track,' 'step,' 'trace'], resonates with the *empty space* (perhaps the very *différance* internal to the mark) that constitutes the hollow of any impression.[54]

By thus radicalizing the usual tendency to attempt to represent the orality of the poem by instead sinking it ever more deeply into printed type, the oral qualities of what are usually referred to as

---

[52] On Imagisme/Vorticism, see Ezra Pound, "A Retrospect," and "Vorticism," in Ezra Pound, *Early Writings: Poems and Prose*, ed. Ira B. Nadel (New York: Penguin, 2005), 253–65, 278–91; for uses of the Chinese character, see Ezra Pound, *The Cantos of Ezra Pound*, 3rd printing (New York: New Directions, 1996), 261, 563, 591.

[53] Olson, *The Maximus Poems*, 298.

[54] See Joseph Bosworth and T. Northcote Toller, *An Anglo-Saxon Dictionary* [online edition], comp. Sean Christ and Ondřej Tichý, Faculty of Arts, Charles University in Prague, http://bosworth.ff.cuni.cz/021193, s.v. *last.*

"digressions" in the poem take a marked typographical shape, and are marked off from the main body-text in Meyer's original typescript by a printed horizontal line. This seems to give license to stitch supplemental material into the extant poem, such as Meyer's account of the "The Bear's Son" — a folk re-telling of a *Beowulf*-narrative analogue from the Old Icelandic *Hrolf's saga kraka* which Meyer incorporates into the poem itself as if it were a digression within *Beowulf* and not ancillary material customarily reserved for an appendix in a critical edition. [55] The practice recalls the philological inserts folded into certain poems by Pound, Olson, Duncan, and Zukofsky, [56] and strongly echoes Olson's *Maximus*, which includes an inventory of supplies needed by particular European settlers in Massachusetts during their first winter.[57]

Meyer's translation of the episode of Herebald and Hæthcyn even includes a chart of comparative etymology to hook the two Old English names into Old Norse mythology:

HOTHcyn
HOTHr

BALDr
HereBALD

Here, Herebald and Hæthcyn are brothers to Hygelac (later to be king in Wedermark at the time of Beowulf's journey to Heorot). Herebald's accidental death (by a stray arrow) comes at the hand of his brother Hæthcyn, whose death during a raid on the Swedes leads to Hygelac's kingship. This song-as-chart gives each brother's name

---

[55] Compare with G.N. Garmonsway, Jacqueline Simpson, and Hilda Ellis Davidson, trans., *Beowulf And Its Analogues* (New York: Dutton, 1971).

[56] See Michael Davidson, "'From the Latin *Speculum*': Ezra Pound, Charles Olson, and Philology," in Michael Davidson, *Ghostlier Demarcations: Modern Poetry and the Material World* (Berkeley: University of California Press, 1997), 94–115.

[57] Charles Olson, "14 MEN STAGE HEAD WINTER 1624/5," in Olson, *The Maximus Poems*, 122.

on the top and bottom, and the Norse cognate of the main part of each name in the center: Baldr and Hothr, proper names from the Old Icelandic Elder (or 'Verse') *Edda*. The linguistically pan-Germanic element in each name is given in capital letters while the element specific to the Anglo-Saxon or Norse names appears in lowercase, arranged with the distinctive Norse nominal case-marker –*r* appearing like a hinge before the line in the center (almost as if an arithmetic problem). The lowercase Anglo-Saxon elements appear diagonally opposite to each other, bottom right and upper left. The translation thus calls attention to a much larger and longer medieval Germanic literary history — gesturing towards the complicated relation of *Beowulf* to Scandinavian culture. This chart foregrounds the translation's printed-ness in terms of a more complex history of writing, as a way to register *Beowulf's* complex relation to orality but also recalling Anglo-Saxon inscriptions: consider these enigmatic graphic marks (like runes) whose concrete shape on the page faintly echoes Anglo-Saxon ornamental scroll-work which can be elaborated in a manner similar to Hrothgar's "reading" of the runes on the sword-hilt Beowulf snatches from the lake.[58] The chart thus underscores the capacity for *Beowulf* to appear as a modern poem: the Old English poem already harbors the figure of a complicated concrete textuality similar to the one used by its twentieth-century translation.

Meyer's translation of the account by the *scop* in Heorot of the Finn and Hengest episode strangely casts a scene of poetry as oral performance in one of the translation's most visually intricate passages:

---

[58] Anina Seiler, "Factual and Fictional Inscriptions: Literacy and the Visual Imagination in Anglo-Saxon England" (paper presented at the biennial meeting of the International Society of Anglo-Saxonists, University of Wisconsin-Madison, August 2, 2011). Seiler argues that "reading" an inscription in Anglo-Saxon England involved not merely pronouncing the very few (often runic) characters carved into a given surface, but also extemporaneously elaborating on the narrative they encode.

                    song
                    sung
                    sing
                    er's
                    saga

          ended: joy rose
             bench rows
             noise boys brought
                        wine in
             wonderous
                   cups
             Wealhltheow

          wore a golden crown

Critic Edward B. Irving, Jr. once considered the possibility that the editing of Old English texts might productively employ the typographically visual innovations of twentieth-century poetry in order to deal with the problems that arise in presenting Old English verse in print.[59] Meyer instead demonstrates the potential for a little bit of careful arrangement of print and typography to bring out visually oriented possibilities latent in the Old English in translation. The song about a singer finishing a song is here deeply entrenched within print conventions, relying on enjambment on the level of the morpheme and syllable (i.e., sing/ er's) to produce a thin rectangle of type. Ironically, it is a set of very medieval Germanic words hovering in a semantic field related to orality that constructs this typographically striking rectangle (*song* and *sung* remain almost identical to their Old English ancestors, *singer* is obviously related, and *saga* is attested in Old English, meaning "saying, story,

---

[59] See Edward B. Irving, Jr., "Editing Old English Verse: The Ideal," in *New Approaches to Editing Old English Verse*, eds. Sarah Larratt Keefer and Katherine O'Brien O'Keeffe (Cambridge: D.S. Brewer, 1998), 14.

statement"). [60] And playfully, this most typographically charged passage rings out with the famous aural device of Anglo-Saxon poetry: alliteration. The alliteration occurs not only in terms of the sounds read aloud, but also in the visual shape of each initial *s* moving down the left side of the column of text — excepting that of the line consisting entirely of "er's," in which the *s* appears alternately at the end of the line, stitching the surrounding lines into a piece in the way that sound-alliteration stitches together half-lines in Old English verse. The staggered lines below continue to stitch heavy aural effects into intricate typographical shape, in a manner recalling a passage of Zukofsky's *"A"* in homage to William Carlos Williams:

> reach
> C
> a cove—
> call it
> Carlos:
>
> smell W
> double U
> two W's ,
> ravine and
> runnel . . . [61]

Meyer's passage offers us the pun on "rose" and "rows'" (recalling Niedecker's "very veery") [62] and the rhyme "noise boys," which interleaves with the more traditional sounding alliteration of "boys brought" — a phrase that also interestingly casts the Old English *byrelas* [plural of *byrel*, l. 1161: 'cup-bearers,' 'stewards'] into the precise detail of "boys." The alliteration on the *w* in *wine, wonderous,*

---

[60] Bosworth and Toller, *An Anglo-Saxon Dictionary*, s.v. *sang, singen* (pp. *sungen*), and *saga*.

[61] Louis Zukofsky, *A-17*, in Zukofsky *"A"*, 384.

[62] Lorine Niedecker, "We are what the seas," in Niedecker, *Collected Poems*, 240: "We are what the seas/ have made us // longingly immense // the very veery / on the fence."

Weahltheow, wore and *crown* even more heavily echoes the aural effects of Anglo-Saxon prosody. The stitchings of sound already present in the Old English text, corresponding as they do in letterforms to visual rhymes, present on their own a set of "dots" ready to be rearranged for the reader as shape.

The Shock of Permission

Writing to David Hadbawnik, Meyer offers a statement which functions at once as an insightful critical appraisal of the difficulty of *Beowulf*, an explanation of the preoccupation of his translation with material textuality, and a very partial sense of why he translated a long Anglo-Saxon poem when he did:

> You know the elephant in the room is that *Beowulf* is really an odd work, an anomaly right from the start. Single extant manuscript, jumbled narrative, murky transition from oral to written, etc. etc. In the early 70s no one was interested in that kind of textuality. Well, maybe in their own way, the French were. Certainly not Americans. From this, my present vantage, that was just what appealed to me.[63]

Just as the dating of *Beowulf* and the temporality of the unique Anglo-Saxon text in relation to the possible oral histories of the poem as we have it remain points of controversy, the temporalities of Meyer's translation are multiple and strange. Meyer's translation already belongs at least to these two times: the time of its composition forty years ago, and this time now of its wider print publication. Meyer's pastiche of varying twentieth-century poetics produces a second crux. As Peter Nicholls notes, the fact of the publication of Pound's *Cantos* well into the 1960s as well as the long careers of the Objectivists (including long periods in which certain of them did not write) extend the practice of modernism well into the 1970s and bring at least "some disorder to a chronology which likes to see 'modernism' expiring before the Second World War."[64]

---

[63] Thomas Meyer, interview with David Hadbawnik (in this volume).
[64] Nicholls, "Modernising modernism," 42, 44.

Critics tend to view Zukofsky's modernism as part of a generation entirely previous to that of Olson, and foundational essays on "postmodern" American verse tend to locate Olson as the epitome of their subject (as Olson himself is often credited with early use of the term "post-modern" to describe himself and his practices).[65] But Olson and Zukofsky were born merely days apart and their partially resonant poetics flourished contemporaneously despite their mutual avoidance of each other.[66] In the midst of all of this, *Beowulf* remains an early medieval poem in Old English. The *Beowulf* of this volume attempts to embrace modernism while it moves beyond it, and at the same time it remains ineluctably an Anglo-Saxon poem and also entirely anterior to the possibility of such desires.

However, as Olson writes, "the weakness of poems is what they do not include," and it is by this virtue that the publication of this translation now recalls a moment of innovation in poetics and demonstrates their pertinence to thinking about *Beowulf* now.[67] Accordingly, Meyer explains that "permission, as Robert Duncan might have it, for the inconsistent formalities all throughout my *Beowulf* was granted directly by Pound's 'Propertius' where he runs the gamut from Victorian mediaeval to H.L. Menken wise-cracking."[68] In Duncan's "Often I am permitted to return to a meadow" (the first poem of the book *The Opening of the Field*, which inaugurated Duncan's engagement with Field Poetics in print), it is a "meadow . . . that is not mine, but is a made place," which famously

---

[65] See David Antin, "Modernism and Postmodernism: Approaching the Present in American Poetry," *boundary 2* 1.1 (1972): 98–133; Charles Altieri, "From Symbolist Thought to Immanence: The Ground of Postmodern American Poetics," *boundary 2* 1.3 (1973): 605–642; and Paul A. Bové, *Destructive Poetics: Heidegger and Modern American Poetry* (New York: Columbia University Press, 1980), esp. xi, 217–81. For an example of Olson's very early use of the term "post-modern" to refer to himself, see *Letters for Origin: 1950-1956*, ed. Albert Glover (New York: Paragon House, 1988), 102.

[66] Stephen Fredman, "'And All Now Is War': George Oppen, Charles Olson, and the Problem of Literary Generations," in DuPlessis and Quartermain, *The Objectivist Nexus*, 286–93.

[67] Olson, *Projective Verse II*, 35.

[68] Thomas Meyer, interview with David Hadbawnik (in this volume).

forms "a place of first permission." As such a place, Meyer's *Beowulf* functions as a topography of forces and trajectories which harbor *Beowulf* as having always been a part of the phenomenon of the twentieth-century avant-garde long-poem. This is not merely a matter of obstructive or "difficult" aesthetics, but of lending to *Beowulf* what Duncan called the "permission poetry gives to the felt world."[69]

Brooklyn & Cleveland[70]

---

[69] Robert Duncan, *The H.D. Book*, eds. Michael Bough and Victor Coleman (Berkeley: University of California Press, 2010), 13.
[70] I would like to thank David Hadbawnik, Roy Liuzza, Haruko Momma, and Eileen Joy for their help with this Introduction.

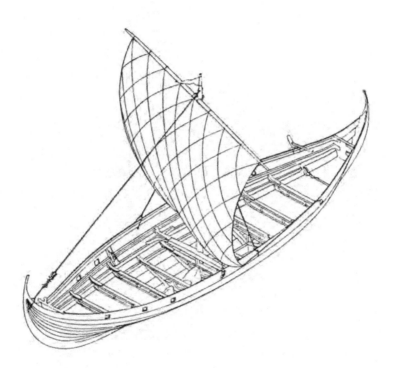

OVERSEA

being the first book of

BEOWULF

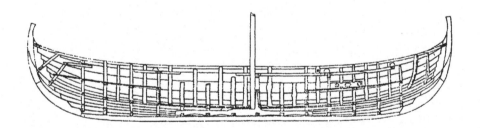

OVERSEA is a translation of lines
1 through 1887, following Fr. Klaeber,
Beowulf and the Fight at Finnsburg,
3rd edition (1950). The second section,
HOMELANDS, completes that text
up to line 3182.

 FOREFIT

HEY now hear

      what spears of Danes
in days of years gone
      by did, what deeds made
their power their glory —

      their kings & princes:

SCYLD SCEFING,
        wretched foundling,

      grew under open skies & in him glory thrived
      & all who threatened his meadhall ran in terror
      & all neighboring nations brought him gold
         following whaleroads.

BEOWULF,
      this good king's son

      grew glorious in the heart of all Scandinavia,
      born to keep his fathers' rule & answer
      his people's need & his gifts brought trust,

        men to stand by him in war, in old age —

      the tribe thrives with each man's rewarded deed.

Scyld's hour came,
his strength went unto his God's keeping

His beloved men carried out his last request,
they bore their king to the shores of the land he long ruled,

to the sea's surge & harbor where
a ringprowed, kingly vessel tossed,
icecrusted, keen to set off.

They laid his glorious, beloved frame amidship,
against the mast & covered it with treasure, trappings

from the realm's farthest reaches,
weapons of war, armor, sword & byrne
set upon his breast.

The seas have never possessed a better geared keel than that.
The riches his people bestowed matched those cast off with him

as a child
in his beginnings
alone upon waves.

They flew a flag woven with golden threads high above his head
& then let the waters bear him unto Ocean's arms away from their

grief & sad hearts. No counselor
nor warrior can say for sure where
that cargo will arrive.

 FIT ONE

& THEN

> Beowulf
of the Scyldings

succeeded his departed
father & lord to rule that
country many years

well known, well loved

& his son, grim, gray

HEALFDENE
lifelong light
of the Scyldings

bore two sons & two daughters
by all counts:

HEOROGAR & HROTHGAR
& good Helga
> & Yrse   (was it?

>> . . . Onela the Swede's
>> queenconsort?)

Luck in battle
            brought Hrothgar
friends,
            kinsmen ready to serve him,
young blood flocked to join his band,
            swell his ranks.

            Then it came to him
to command to be built a great lodge
& men undertook this work erecting
a meadhall larger than any they had
ever seen or heard of

                        under whose beams
all gifts God gave him
                        (all but
the landshare & lifebreath
He provides for men)
                        would be dealt out
to young & old alike.

& tribe upon tribe arrived from all
throughout Midgarth to girt, to decorate
this meetingplace
                        & despite its size
their work went quickly.

            That greatest hall
stood ready for Hrothgar's lips & hands
to shape its name, fulfill its promise:

            He called it Heorot
& there bestowed rings & riches upon
his warriors as they feasted under
towering, cliffhigh
                        gablehorns.

One day not long off

    fire
will burn those walls
    flames

will temper hatred's blade,
     cleave
son & fatherinlaw —
but this has yet to be.

    The dark rang.
    The new hall's
       noise fell
upon tortured ears. In

    the dark dwelt
      a beast who ached as he heard

loud sweet

      harp notes

          cast song's sharp shape, craft

       unfold the airs
            & fill the ears

        with all origins —

Where water rings the world's bright fields
     sun & moon lend their glory's light
as lamps for men on land
                         & tree leaf &
     limb deck out earth's every fold
          as breath quickens
each creaturekind.

          Hrothgar's men
          enjoyed happy lives
          at Heorot & then

     the Hellfiend's raids began . . .

That grim ghostbeast called Grendel
dwelled on doomed ground in demonrealms &
made swamp & moor his stronghold. He stalked
those borderlands one of the banished kin of
outcast Cain, Abel's killer, Almighty God
condemned to live beyond mankind.

     Cain's crime fathered an evil brood:

          ents & orcs & elves
          & giants who
                         long ago
          waged war on God
          & won themselves
          His reward.

 FIT TWO

NIGHT came. He went
to check out those Danes
boozing at home in their
big house & pay them a call.

    He found
them snoozing like fat, well
fed babies safe from boogies.

    BANG! like a flash
that hard hearted, grim, greedy,
sick thing snatched 30 sleeping
Danes &
    jiggetyjig ran home again,
fists full of blood candy.

& then
    dawn's first
     light lit
    what Grendel
     did

       hid
    none of it
& then

    last night's
    cups brimmed
    with morning
    wept

       tears

An old, renowned king's grief.
An evil ghost's ugly foot print.

Too much pain too soon, too long.
Murder's fearless pattern set

    in less than a night.

Feud   Sin
certain sign clear token
                 Sin   Feud
           out of season   no let up

    Men sought digs
    outside the hall,
    got as far from
    hate's haunt
    as they could.

    One took them all on.
    That greatest of houses
    stood idle.

    12 bitter winters
    taught the Scyldings'
    king each sorrow
    under the sun.

    Tongues wagged, lips
    clacked: Grendel's
    attacks, Hrothgar's
    pain common knowledge.

    No truce, no ransom,
    no glory possible for men,
    seasoned or green,
    at the hands of that
    horrible beast.

Death's dark shadow

hovered over moors,

      plot thickened mist

& never ending night.

      Hell's runes

hid all trails.

      Singlehanded
Hell's fiend held Heorot,
made its cold hearth his home.
Night's dark. Scylding's grief.
That beast knelt before no Lord's
throne.
His deeds went unrewarded.

Men of rank met, asked:

"What runes, what sacrifice
will answer our people's need?"

Priests & chiefs prayed:

"Troll Killer, our god &
 single aid, deliver us!"

Hell dwelled in their hearts, heathen rites
darkened their minds. They knew nothing of

God Almighty, Heaven's Helm, Judge of Deeds.
Pagans deaf to Glory's praises know no solace,

      shove their souls
      into terrorrealms
      unto fires' arms,

      remain unborn.

      Death's day brings
      joy to men
      if they seek peace,

      the Father's arms.

 FIT THREE

NIGHT & day
   care's tides
rose & fell,
    drowned Healfdene's
son. No runes
    stilled storm's
rage. Damned
    wrack, grim doom,
nightfear.

Too much pain too soon, too long.

    Hygelac's thane,
noble, mighty, brave Geat, his
manhood, then ripe, got wind of
Grendel's rampage & decked out
a ship fit to fare waves, said
"I'll track swans' path to seek
that good king in need of men."

Friends & counselors
  unable to turn him from
his journey
  urged him on,
drew his sorts, checked omens
for the brave, beloved prince.

He picked a company from the best men he could find.

15 sought seawood,
led to land's edge
by seawise warrior,

set keel to breakers,

left
    shore's ledge,
leapt
    churned sand.

Sea surge bore forth
    bright cargo:

weapons, trappings,
hearts keen to man
    timberbound,
wavelapped,
    windwhipped,
foamthroated bird.

        Ship floated. Sail filled.
        A day & a day prow plowed
        & crew saw bright cliffs,
        steep hills, wide beaches.

        Sea crossed. Land at last.
        Boat moored. Byrnes shook.

Weder men thanked God for an easy voyage over waves.

Glint of shieldbosses

    across gangplanks

caught in coastguard's eye

    on seawall at seawatch

flashed upon his mind,

    pricked his brain.

"Who goes there? Why? What are they up to?"

Hrothgar's thane rode his horse down to the beach.

    Spear's great wood quaked in his hand.

He drew his quick breath, steadied himself & said:

"Who are you in your armor & your mail,
brought by tall keel along the sea's road
upon wide waves? For years at land's end
I've watched the shore for enemy armies
come by ship to invade & raid us Danes
& never seen shielded men arrive so openly.

Yet I've had no warning, no news of you,
no orders from my kinsmen to let you pass.

& I've seen no greater earl on earth than
one of you appears to be,
        no mere hallman
glamorized by dazzling armor, strengthened
by weapons alone,
      unless his looks weave lies,
he has no equal.

    But now before you take
another step on Danish soil I must be told
where you sailed from & why. For all I know
you foreigners & seafarers may be spies, so
answer my simple question, haste is best:

Where have you come from?"

 FIT FOUR

"WE   are Geats!"

Crew's captain & chief
unlocked his wordhoard,
his answer rolled from
his tongue:

"Ecgtheow,

my father,
all folk knew well,
the flower of his kinship
survived many winters
before it faded
ripened by many years

leaving his memory
to thrive in the minds
of all wisemen
throughout wide earth."

55

We come with warm hearts to seek Healfdene's son.
Show us goodwill, give us godspeed on our guest errand
unto your illustrious Danish lord.
Our journey's rime will soon be no secret, I think.

You know — if rumors we've heard hold true —
that some scourge among Scyldings
shapes its hate's deeds by dead of night,
twisting its terror's strange, violent designs
from living men's humiliation & dead men's blood.

I bring buried in the wide ground of my heart
seeds of an answer for brave, old Hrothgar: how
he might overcome this fiend, untwist the tight net
its evil weaves & cast good fortune's change,
stilling care's swelling tides —

                if it is any longer possible —

for otherwise forever after suffering & sorrow
shall be every day's necessity at good Heorot,
best of halls, for as long as it endures upon
                its lofty heights."

Coastguard on horseback
cleared his throat,
unfaltering officer spoke:
                    "As any clever
shieldbearer in his right mind would, I've
weighed your words & deeds & now think you
a troop loyal to Scyldings' lord. Bear forth
your weapons in battledress, I'll be your guide
& leave my men to guard your freshtarred boat
from enemies, keeping its curved wood keel
safe on sand until it's ready to bear
its beloved band
                    whom fate allows to weather
war's storm whole
                    back across sea's streams
to Wederland."

They set off, their widehulled boat at rest,
rope & anchor held it fast.

                    Gold swine emblems
gleamed above cheekguards —
                    inlaid, firehard
tusk & snout,
                    twisted tail.
                    Bristled boar:

warhearts' blazon, lifebreaths' protector.

Together men marched.
Their quick pace brought them
in sight of

        gilt, glint,

splendor,

        timbered hall,

mighty king's seat,

        house

most prime

        under heaven

in earthdwellers' minds
whose fires' light lit

        many lands.

        Coastguard pointed out

        the direct route to that

bright lodge, lighthearted men's home,

        turned his horse & said:

"It is time now for me to get back. May
the allruling Father's mercy keep you
& your mission sound.
                I go to the sea
to resume my watch against our enemies."

 . FIT FIVE. .

STONE

paved
    street

    straight
track

    byrnes'
shine

    bright
        hard
        hand
    linked
rings

        war
        gear
songs

    horror
    armor

warriors entered the hall.
Set their wide, hardbossed shield
together against the wall,
sat down on a bench.

                   Warbyrnes clanked.
       Graytipped
               ashwood spears gathered.
        Seamen
             ironclad, fighters
     Weapondecked.

             A king's thane
asked them their bloodlines:

"Where do you come from with plated shields,
gray mailshirts, grim warhelmets & that
heap of spears? I am Hrothgar's messenger
& officer. I've never seen a braver looking
foreign troop — you must seek Hrothgar
out of wide hearts, not out of wreck or exile."

Answer's words came
loudly from under
the bold, lordly
Weder leader's helmet:

           "We share Hygelac's board."

BEOWULF

my name

"I would like to tell

your renowned king

Healfdene's son,

my errand myself

should his majesty

grant us audience."

Wulfgar,
          Vendel's chief,
                              whose
heart's
          prowess & wisdom
                                        many
knew,
          paused & replied:

"I will ask as you request

Scyldings' lord, Dane's friend

& ringgiver, our glorious king,

about your journey

& will all speed return with

the good man's answer."

Quickly
    the war hero
trained
    in protocol
went to
    where old, gray Hrothgar,
    the Danish lord,
    sat with his retinue.
    Face to face he addressed
    his protector:

"Here are Geatmen
come from afar
over wide ocean.
Beowulf, warrior
chief, wishes to
have words with you.

Gracious Hrothgar,
do not refuse them.
Their array commands
an earl's esteem —
indeed, their leader
is a strong man."

 FIT SIX

WORDS   welled in Hrothgar, Scyldings' helm:

> "I knew him when he was a boy,
> his father's name was Ecgtheow
> to whom the Geat Hrethel gave
> his only daughter as a wife —
> now his son comes to us,
> a trusted friend. Our seafarers
> who took Geats' gifts of thanks
> say his hand's grip has the fire
> of 30 men's battlestrength.
> It is my hope & joy that Holy God
> in His mercy sends him to us Danes
> to unwind Grendel's evil gyre.
> I will reward his heart's might
> with goods & treasures. Quick now,
> call them in, the entire kinband
> & give them words of welcome
> from all Danish peoples."

Wulfgar went to the hall door, called to them outside:

> "My glorious lord, the Dane's king,
> tells me to tell you he knows
> your heritage. Stronghearted men
> from across sea's swells, here
> you are welcome. You may see
> Hrothgar in your array, under war's
> grim masks but leave your shield
> boards & wooden slaughtershafts
> to await your words' outcome."

The powerful leader rose,
splendid ranks around him.

& ordered some of his band
to stay & guard their gear.

He led the rest into Heorot.
The warhard warrior stood

under its rafters
at its hearth

his
shirt

smith
crafted
links

brilliant
net

byrne
glitter
shone

his
words

a dark echo from
under his helmet:

"Hail Hrothgar,
I am Hygelac's kin & thane
my acts of youth were
glory's deeds
Grendel's outrage
was no secret
in Geats' lands.
Seafarers told our warriors
this best of houses
stood idle, useless
when heaven hid
day's light.
They urged me to
seek
wise
Hrothgar.
They know me, have seen me come
from battle drenched in
fiend's blood
dead ents
(5 prisoners)

watched me slay krakens
on waves at night
my life in danger
the acts of
those creatures I crushed
sealed their own fate

Weders' revenge

& now I have a score to settle with Grendel

troll
beast."

"Having come this far I beg you, Scyldings' protector,
warriors' shelter & people's friend, do not deny me
             this one favor:

Let me & my strong band clean up Heorot by ourselves.

I've discovered that this reckless beast uses no weapons,
so to Hygelac my lord's delight I'll take this fiend on
             barehanded,

fight him tooth & nail for life & let God's doom name
             the loser death hauls off.

If Grendel gets the upper hand no doubt he'll make a meal
             of us Geats,

he's tasted manhood's flower in this hall many times before.

             If I die dig me no grave
for I'll be that monster's supper, slaughter salted,
             gore sauced.

             Alone on his moors
he'll pick his teeth with my bones.

             No you won't have to build my barrow.

             If battle claims me
send Hygelac my byrne, this good mailshirt made by Weland
             that Hrethel left.

             What will be will be."

 FIT SEVEN

WORDS   welled in Hrothgar, Scyldings' helm:

"Indebted, in mercy, Beowulf, my friend,
you come to us. Alone, your father
struck a great feud with the Wylfings
when his strong hand slew Heathlaf.

His own kin, the Weders, dare not
harbor him for fear of war. So he
sought us honored Scyldings just
as my reign of the Danes began.

Young as I was, I ruled a wide land
& a hoard of fine warriors. Heregar,
my older brother, Healfdene's son,
my better, had not been dead long

when I settled the Wylfings' feud
by sending them antique treasures
in payment for spilt blood & Ecgtheow
pledged allegiance to me in return."

69

                    "My heart grieves
when I speak of the damage
Grendel's hate, plots & lightning
raids have done,

when I think how my halltroops,
my fighting men thin out, swept
by fate into Grendel's evil gyre,
& how easily God could end
                 these mad deeds.

Often in the hall
beer filled warriors boast in cups
that they will wait out the night, pit
their sharp swordedges against
Grendel's attack.
                But when
morning stains the meadhall's gore
& wet blood gleams on bench & plank
daylight finds few left alive,
death hauls away the loved & trusted.

    Now sit. Eat. Unbind your thoughts.
    Then tell us the tales of glory your
    hearts bring to mind."

Room was made on a bench in the beerhall
for all the Geats. They went & sat there
glowing with strength. A cupbearer came
with an ornate alebeaker in his hands to
pour them bright, sweet drink.

Now & then
      Heorot rang
           with songs

the poet's
      clear voice
           & heroes' joys

swelled into noise,
      shouts & cries of

no minor company,
      Danes & Weders.

 FIT EIGHT

UNFERTH,   Ecglaf's son,

                         who sat at

the Scylding lord's feet broke

the hush he caused

                         when he stood

to utter baited words,

                         battlerunes:

(This fuss over a seafarer's journey
annoyed him: he granted no man in
Midgarth greater praise for deeds
done under heaven than he received.)

"Are you the Beowulf who swam a race
on open seas with Breca,

                         tested tides
out of pride
                 & because of a rash boast
risked your life in deep water,

                                      who
no man,
           friend or foe, could turn from
this adventure's danger?"

73

"You swam,

       sea's foam wreathed your arms,
your hands

       thrashed their way along sea's roads as
Ocean's fork

       tossed you into sea's boiling floods &
winter's waves crashed upon sea's streams. Water
held your body

       7 nights

       when Breca's greater strength
gained him the lead.

       At dawn he climbed
from sea to shore onto Heathoraemas' land
then made his way home to Brondings' fair, peaceful
capitol,

       to the cities & wealth he rules,
to the people who loved him.

       Beanstan's son fulfilled his boast.

       No matter how well you've weathered
       battle's storm or withstood war's
       grim rage
       I don't give you a fighting
chance of surviving one night in or near
       Grendel's grip."

Beowulf, Ecgtheow's son, quietly replied:

> "Unferth, my friend,
> your beer speaks for you
>
> The truth
> in all your talk
> about Breca's adventure

is that no man's strength matched my own.

> Let me
> make it clear:

when we were boys we made a pact to pitch
our youth upon Ocean's prong & challenged
his swift seas' rough waves, *not* each other.

> Breca never
> gained a stroke on me
> nor tried to.

For 5 nights bitter cold rolling waves
dashed us about under black skies headlong
into deadly grim northern gales. We swam
with hard, naked swords in our hands until
the flood separated us.
                    Its waves grew fiercer
rousing sea fishes' anger.
                    The knit of my hard
handlinked sark slung to my body, covered
my breast with a guilded byrne's protection.
                    Then a scavenger
dragged me under, a fiend's tight grip plunged
me to Ocean's floor but my sword point, granted
a direct hit, pierced the monster, my hand
guided that great seabeast into battle's storm."

75

 FIT NINE

"NOT   once

    but many times

my good sword

    saw fit to slash

not one

    but many

bloated

    whale bellies

whose

    juices ran

stirred

    by thoughts of

sitting

    down to

a deep

    sea board

laid

    with me.

Morning

    found them

hacked

    by blades

washed

    by waves

ashore

    asleep

with death

    never to trouble

ocean

    goers again."

77

"Light came over the East,

                God's bright beacon.

Sea swells stilled.

                I saw headlands,

windswept hills.

                Often fate leaves
            a strong man unscathed:
                such was my lot,
              my hilt notched up
                9 monsters'
                  death

No man I know of

                fought harder or

found himself

                in worse straits

by night in sea streams.

                Under sky's arc
            I escaped hatred's grip
                  alive,
            flood & tide brought me
              to Finns' land
                exhausted."

"Unferth,   if there are tales like that about
            your craft in battle or
            your sword's terror
they go untold. Forgive me if I boast but
            the deeds you & Breca have done
            have yet to match my own
            though murder patterns

            your bright blade with
            your brother's blood —
            your cleverness will feed Hell's fires.

Grendel's evil gyre could have never spun
            so much humiliation or
            so much horror
in your king's Heorot if your heart & mind were
            as hard in battle
            as you claim.

            But now the beast knows
there's no feud or swordstorm to fear from
            your people, the glorious Danes.

            He eats you Scyldings alive,
no mercy stems his appetite, his lust your death.

            But soon I'll show him
what this Geat can do in battle & by dawn tomorrow

            all who wish to
            may walk to this meadhall
            free from fear by morning light

            when sun's bright byrne
            shines in the South."

79

Glad words heard
by brave, gray-haired, bright
Danes' chief & folkshepherd:
needed aid found,

Beowulf's promise.

Warriors' laughter,
melodies sound,
cheers of joy.

Wealhtheow, Hrothgar's queen, gold clad lady & good wife,
greeted the men & passed the cup in proper fashion, first
to the Danes' beloved guardian, bidding him drink this beer
in joy. The victorious king drank & ate with lust. Then
the Helmings' lady made her rounds with the treasured cup
to young & old alike in hall's every part & when the ring
decked, rich hearted queen came to Beowulf she greeted
the Geats' leader & wisely thanked her God that her wish was
fulfilled: here was a hero to trust to free her house
from evil. The fierce fighter took the meadcup from
Wealhtheow. Raising it, Beowulf, Ecgtheow's son, his blood
hot with the thought of forthcoming battle, spoke:

"I said when I set out to sea
seated in my boat with my company
that I would answer your people's
prayers at once or cringe
crushed in the fiend's grip.
& so I will — or meet my days'
end in this meadhall."

The Geat's promise pleased the good folkqueen,
the gold clad wife went & sat by her lord.
Once more the hall hears

> brave speech,
>
> troops' joy,
>
> victory's noise

Healfdene's son soon rose to go to his rest.
From sunrise to sunset, in day's light
his high hall was safe, the raids on it just
plans hatched in the monster's brain. But when
dark blacked out things

> a shadeshape would
>
> come & glide like a
>
> shadow under skies.

All stood.
King & hero saluted each other.
Hrothgar wished Beowulf luck & with these words
turned his hall over to him:
"Never since my hand could lift a shield have I
entrusted this Danes' lodge to any man but you.
Guard & keep this best of homes in glory's name,
make it the scene of courage in wrath's wake,
survive this work & your wants won't lack fulfillment."

 FIT TEN

HROTHGAR   & his men left the hall.

The Scyldings' chief & protector

      sought his queen

Wealhtheow —

     her arms in his bed.

The glorious king, as all heard,

had appointed a hallguard

to meet Grendel —

his entwatch was a favor,

a service rendered unto Danes' lord.

The Geats' leader placed his trust

in his own great strength & God's grace.

He took off his iron byrne,
lifted the helmet from his head
& handed them to his servant
along with his engraved blade,
best of swords, telling the boy
to take care of this gear.

Before he climbed up to his bed
the Geat, Beowulf said:

"I believe in *my* battlecraft
as much as Grendel believes in *his*

therefore my sword's blow will not
make his waking sleep although it could.

Despite his evil reputation, he knows
nothing of the shattered shield

so tonight I set aside my sword
If he dares to fight weaponless

let him come & let wise God, Holy Lord,
grant glory to him who deserves it."

He laid down.
His cheek pressed the pillow.

Throughout
      the hall
bold
   seamen
      sunk
into uneasy
     sleep
All hope
   of homecoming
faded

(the good earth that fed them,
their peaceful city, their
friends, kin)
    into dreams.
None could count
    the number
of Danes slaughtered
under this lodge's
    gablehorns.

Yet the lord twisted
    victory,
threads of
   His mercy's aid,
into the Weders' battleweb:

one man's
   craft would overcome

the fiend's might.

85

       Truth made manifest:
mighty God's
           wide mind wields
all mankind.

       The shadow came,

       stalked, pierced

       night's dark.

       God's

       will alone would allow

       the ghostbeast's void

       to swallow these warriors.

Sleep broke all but

one man's

watch, anger flared in him with rage —

       his enemy's arrival,

       their battle's outcome

       marked time.

❧ FIT ELEVEN ❧

GRENDEL   came

              from his moors

                  hid by hillfog,

              God's curse

                  embedded in his hide,

             to set an evil snare

                  for one certain man

             in that high hill.

Under clouded skies he stalked within clear sight of
that gold plated structure, that winehouse of men.

This wasn't

      the first visit

he'd paid Hrothgar

      but never before

in all his days

      or since

had he had such hard luck: those warriors were waiting there.

87

Joyless, up to the lodge

the raider came.

His fist no sooner hit the doors than
the firehard bolt laid across them
snapped in two,
                    they dropped open
like a broken jaw.
                    The chaosfiend
walked in,
                    stomped across the polished floor.

His heart's hate flashed in his eyes
like the ugly blaze of a burning barn.

His heart leapt to see the scene before him:
a heap of warriors, juicy arms, trunks & legs.
His mouth watered at the thought of them
ripped from limb to limb,
                    limp & lifeless.

(This was to be the last night fate laid men upon his plate.)

The eyes of Hygelac's kin watched the wicked raider
execute his quick attack:
                    without delay,
snatching his first chance,
                    a sleeping warrior,
he tore him in two,
                    chomped muscle, sucked veins'
gushing blood,
                    gulped down his morsel, the dead man,
chunk by chunk,
                    hands, feet & all.

& then

footstephandclawfiendreachmanbedquicktrick
beastarmpainclampnewnotknownheartrunflesho
feargetawaygonowrunrun

                                   never before had
sinherd feared anything so.

                    ("or cringed crushed . . .

                       or my days' end . . .")
Beowulf stood up straight,
                                 beast in his grip,
his knuckles popped.
                        Ent bent on escape

runwideflatopenswampholessafebadfingerman
squeezeletgowantnotcomesadgobadhallrunrun

                        Rattle,
roar in lordly hall,
                  every Dane's blood,
warrior, earl or servant, froze.

                      Both beast
& man, both guards
                  thrashed furious, frantic.
Building boomed.

It was a miracle
the winehall withstood
their battle,

didn't crash
to the ground
a heap of rubble

Inside & out
smithcrafted ironbands
held its walls fast.

Gilt meadbenches
ripped from floor, tipped,
tossed by flight, yet

wise Scyldings knew no man could wreck
good, bone adorned, antler decked Heorot
— only flames' fathom & fires' scorch
could unlink the skill that built it

A new sound: scream   screech   howl
split the ears of Danes outside.
Yelps heard, terror gripped them.
Hell's slave, God's enemy chanted
horrorsong

        nogoodnokillno
        gonopainopain
        armburnpainono

Beast in the hold of man matchless
in strength & might on Midgarth, in
earth's corners in that day & age.

🎈 FIT TWELVE 🎈

NOTHING   could make earlshelter, Beowulf, let go —
he reckoned deathbringer's quick brought none good.

Swords, heirlooms, old blades hacked at monsterhide.
Men joined the fight to protect their lord & chief.

But none knew the wicked life they sought to stem
was safe from all earthly weapons' glorious powers.

      The beast had cast a spell to stay
      even the best of iron edge's cuts.

Yet in that day & age
            that ghost from another world
would start upon his
            wretched journey back into
distant demonrealms.

      He whose heart feuded with God
      & plotted men's murder
      found that the body that once
      did his bidding no longer obeyed.

      His hand stuck
      fast in the grip of Hygelac's kin.
      Man & monster, mutual enemies
      for as long as they each drew breath.

                    raw wound gaping sinews severed
                    snapped muscles bare bones blood

                                                                    visible agony

                    Hellbeast's shoulder
Beowulf   granted battle's glory.

Grendel   fled for moors & hills,

                    his joyless lair —
                    struck to the quick,
                    his life's lease up
                    his days number nil.

                    Blood
                    storm realized all Danes'
                    wished: Hrothgar's hall

                    cleansed by him who came from afar,
                    delivered from chaos by a strong,
                    wise heart.

                    They rejoiced for
                    that night's work,
                    its glory & valor.

                    Geats' leader made good his boast,
                    cured that sorrow, no small grief,
                    Danes suffered without any choice.

Beowulf   hung the hand, arm & shoulder,

Grendel   's total grasp under roof's sweep,   visible token
                    inside gablehorn's curve.

❧ FIT THIRTEEN ❧

MORNING,
        many warriors
                surrounded the giftlodge.
Chieftains
        fared wide highways
                far & near to see
a wonder:
        the wicked beast's footprints.
All who
        stood where Grendel trod
                felt no grief
for life
        lost along that track
                to Kraken Lake,

        no glorytrail:
                a path of blood
        that traced defeat's flight led
        straight to Monster Mere where
        blood & water boiled — putrid
        waves surged, hot gore poured
        upon whirlpools, ripples of
        slaughter.
                Death's doom swarmed

        to hide that heathen soul,
        home to rest in swamp's peace.

There Hell received its own.

men boys glossy steeds

glad journey

back from the lake

talk

of Beowulf's glory:

"No hand that holds a shield

north or south of here

has greater right to rule

this stretch of land

beneath wide open skies

between two seas

than his, this royal

worthy warrior's —

with no offence meant to great

Hrothgar, a good king!"

Now & then &

     when the road opened out

     into a flat, clear, familiar course

     horses, riders leapt ahead, raced

     each other: battlebrave on bays.

& now & then

     a man

     in whom men's deeds echoed,
                    shifting
     his mind's hoard
         to stir words that
     welled into
         tales, twicetold shapes
     bound by
        his skull's full armor,

     sang a song of Beowulf & told what

     little he knew of Sigemund's tale:

"None know the whole story,
all the ins & outs about
that son of Wael's battles,
brave deeds, broad travel, bloodshed & feuds.

Well, none but his mother's
brother Fitela, like hand
to hilt in battle they fought
thick as thieves as they were, together they slew

more ents than you can count
& when Sigemund died his fame
spread overnight & far & wide
folk talked about the worm he killed all alone,

without his uncle Fitela
he crawled into a ghastly
lair beneath gray rock
where it guarded a hoard big beyond all telling.

By sheer chance with one
blow his noble iron sword
cut clean through the worm's
gem crusted hide & rotten flesh & struck rock

pinning the stinking carcass
against its own cave wall
like a spitted ox to roast
in the flames of its own roar & murdered breath

leaving that monster of a
warrior, Wael's son, to
take his pick of the hoard.
He loaded down his boat, packed his ship's hold

with gold & jewels & black dragon fat sputtered."

"The brave adventures of that warrior's warrior
brought him glory, fame & fortune. As far as
exiles go, Sigemund's the best known. But let's
not forget Heremod, his tale may fade but not his
fights & deeds, they still deserve a song:

>He fell into the hands of Jutes & died
>a quick death — a mercy maybe, an end
>to his long restless wanderings. He'd
>been cast out by his people because when
>he was their king they feared for their
>lives, his willful rule failed to ful-
>fill his wisemen's hopes, his people's
>need: they wanted an end to suffering,
>a king like his father was, a strong pro-
>tector of the Scyldings' hoard, citadel
>& homelands.
>> Sin ate out his heart.
>He was no man's joy — no *Beowulf*!"

Dustclouds, horseraces —
> sun hurried unto noon.

Stouthearted servants went to that high hall
& gawked at the strange thing hung up there.

The good king & renowned ringward himself
came from his bed followed by his lords,

his queen & her ladies. Together that company
strode up the footpath up to their meadhall.

 FIT FOURTEEN

HROTHGAR

climbed the porch steps,
stood between the posts,
looked up to the steep
gilt roof
          at the ghost's
hand & said:

"Let us stop now
          to thank the Almighty,
the Shepherd of Glory,
          for we are beholden:

wonder upon wonder
the power of God's
          eternal hand.

Less than a year ago
          I thought I'd never
live to see an end
          to the blood spilt
in this best of halls:

the gore & hate
of Grendel's hand
washed away."

99

"My wisemen lost all hope.

None could cut the gnarled
roots of grief that clutched
my people's earth or break
the hold of phantoms' glamour.

Now by God's aid a man
succeeds where all our
well laid plans failed.

God bless the woman, alive or dead
whose womb bore this son for mankind!

Now & forever more
I shall love you, Beowulf,
like a son & keep the peace
such a kinship makes

& all you want
of this world
that is in my power to give
shall be yours.

Many lesser men than you
have received my honored gifts
for weaker deeds than yours.

May what you have done here
seal your fame for eternity.
May the Almighty continue
to grant you the success
he gives you now."

Tears in the old man's eyes.

Beowulf, Ecgtheow's son, replied in turn:

"With all goodwill
we undertook a dark work,
dared to cross
         an enigma's path.

How I wish
you'd been there, Hrothgar, to see
the fiend fall
         in full array.

I'd meant to
wrap my arms around him, bind him
to death's bed
         with a bear's,

a beewolf's hug
but his body slipped my grip:
God's will, he
         jerked free.

His last burst
of strength broke my hold
yet he left in
         his tracks

the price of his life:
hand, arm & shoulder —
too narrow an escape
from battle's grasp.

Nothing can heal his wound, he hasn't long to live.
Sin weighs him down, evil binds him, crime stains him.
He awaits the Bright Lord's great judgment, his doom."

101

That noble earl's craft left
Unferth, Ecglaf's son, speechless.
His yelping tongue stopped when
all those warriors stared upon
each finger of that rafterhung
hand, each nail on that heathen
paw a steel spur, a deadly talon.
They agreed, no man's bladeiron,
however good, could touch that fist
of awls, wreck those bloody spikes.

 FIT FIFTEEN

A COMMAND:

quick hands
deck out Hart

men, women
ready the
winehall, guestlodge

gold threads,
webs on
walls, sights to see

That monster marked by his own evil left
that bright but broken building's hinges
sprung but the insides still standing,
held by ironbands. Only the roof remains
all in one piece when he turned to flee,
his life fading fast.

Those who take a stab at cheating death
leap in the dark, try as they may,

the soul of every living being,
each earthdwelling man's child,
must seek its need's necessity.

Its place prepared,
its body comes to rest
fast asleep in its grave,

its feast unfinished.

In due time, the hour right, Healfdene's son arrived.
The king himself wished to join in his hall's feasting.

No greater nor nobler company ever before swelled
the ranks of subjects gathered around their treasuregiver.

Men sat down on benches. Their glory, their wealth,
their joy overflowed. Hrothgar & Hrothulf, great hearted
kin, downed the many expected cups of mead in their hall.

Friends filled high Heorot. Treachery's runes had yet
to score Scyldings' hearts with dark stratagems.

Healfdene's son presented Beowulf
with gifts, victories' rewards:

a gold standard, his battleblazon,

a helmet, a byrne, a sword all saw
held high, carried up to the warrior.

Beowulf drank his cup dry,
thanked the Lord for his hallgifts,

accepting them before the assembly
shameless & unembarrassed.

No show of friendship had ever
been so glorious:
                    4 gold treasures.

No man before had so honored
another upon the alebench.

A wire wound ridge
across the helmet's crown

kept the skull inside safe
from blows of any sword

hammered & ground
to join the shield in

an enemy's hand.

Hrothgar, warriors' shield, ordered
8 gold bridled steeds to be brought
through the yard into the hall: one

a workhorse saddled with a battleseat
marked by a craft that made it treasure,
which Healfdene's son, the high king,

rode on, out to the frontranks' swordplay.
There among the slaughtered & fallen
his renowned strength never failed him.

Ingwines' prince bestowed both horses & weapons
upon Beowulf for his good use.
                              Heroes' hoardward
& famous chief rewarded him with steeds & treasure
for weathering battle's storm.
                              Let no just man
who seeks to speak the truth fault these gifts.

⚫ FIT SIXTEEN ⚫

& EARL'S
      lord gave
each man on meadbench
who crossed the sea with Beowulf
gifts, heirlooms, promised
them gold, bloodmoney for
the man they lost to Grendel.
A small price to pay, his victims
would have been unnumbered if
wise God & one man's heart had not
stood in the way. The Lord still
holds mankind's fate in
His hand: a fact the mind
that plans ahead should heed.
These days a man must endure
both good & bad as long as he
lives in & makes use of
this world.

song & sound from
strung wood strum

harp's joy words
& music linked in

a tale turned to
bind entwine all

hearts at Heorot
& Hrothgar, Healfdene's chief

107

The poet went in & out of
the benchrows & told about

Finn's men, how the Danes'
heroes & Hnaef the Scylding

fell
in a sudden attack
on Frisian fields:

"With good reason
Hildeburh put no trust in Jutes after,
guiltless herself, she lost loved ones,
sons & brothers, to shield woods' clash,
rushed by fate, wounded by spears. O
sad woman.

With good reason
Hoc's daughter wept when morning came
to light destiny's designs. She saw below
bright skies her murdered, slaughtered kin
where once she had known the world's
greatest joys.

That fight claimed all
but a few of Finn's men. There was not
a chance left of finishing that battle
with Hengest upon those grounds or even
of rescuing slaughter's survivors by force,
so a truce was drawn, offered & accepted:"

"Half the lodge
would be cleared
to be their hall & highseat.

Half the rule
would be theirs
to be shared with the Jutes.

The gilded favors of Finn, Folcwada's son,
rich gifts, rings & treasures,
would be as much the Danes'
as the Frisians' when
cheer honored their beerhall.

A treaty both sides
promised to keep
without fail. Without hesitation
Finn pledged an oath to Hengest:
Slaughter's survivors would be treated
as his wisemen advised, that is,
with honor.

No man would break that peace by
word or deed or with malice mention
that priceless act, that is, out of necessity,
they'd sworn allegiance to
their own ringgiver's slayer, in other words,

the memory of that feud that a Frisian's
careless, hasty words might stir up could
be settled by the sword's edge alone."

"Pyre readied.

          Hoargold brought.

Warriors in

          funnelgear, best

Scyldingmen

          & no lack of

bloodstained mailshirts or guilded
swine, ironhard boar, or bodies
injured, destroyed by battlewounds

          on that firepile.

Hildeburh ordered her sons' flesh,
blood & bones committed to Hnaef's
funeral pyre's flames laid arm to
arm, shoulder by shoulder.

          Dirges, chants, keening
O sad woman.

          Warriors lifted up,

slaughter's fires licked the skies,
roared before his barrow.

Skulls popped, gashes burst, sword
bites spat blood:

          fire's greed
glutted by men battle snatched from
both sides,
          shaken free of life."

FIT SEVENTEEN

" & THEN

the friendless warriors went back
to Frisia to find the homes & uplandtowns
they'd left.

But Hengest stayed behind,
shared that hard winter with Finn,

homesick, yet

storms, winds churned, swelled the seas

his slender keel would have to cross.

Ice locked

waves in winter's grasp

until the new year came

bringing man

soft weathers, as always,

even now, each season

takes its turn."

111

"When earth shook winter
from her bright lap

revenge sprang up
in the exile's heart.

Where sea & homethoughts
dwelt plans to provoke

an incident grew: an iron
sword in the stranger's heart.

So when Hunlafing laid
a bright blade (that best

of swords, that edge all Jutes
knew well) upon his lap

Hengest did what any man
in this world would . . .

Finn died in his own home
killed by swordblows

when Gudlaf & Oslaf talked
of the attack & sorrow their men

met at their seajourney's end,
blaming Finn for most of it.

A restless heart can't be pent
up in a man's breast for long.

That hall ran red with enemy blood."

"King Finn slain
amidst his bodyguard,
his queen seized,
his house sacked,   pins
everything worth taking   neckrings
carried off by Scyldings,   carved gems
loaded in their ship
to cross the sea   & his wife

brought back to Danes,
returned to her people."

              song
              sung
              sing
              e r' s
              saga

ended: joy rose
        bench rows'
        noise boys brought
                    wine in
        wonderous
              cups
        Weahltheow

wore a golden crown
& went to where two
good men, nephew &
uncle (brother's son,
father's brother) sat,

each still true to the other,
the peace between them firm.

113

Unferth, spokesman, sat there too
at the feet of Scyldings' lord

together with a company that put
their trust in Hrothgar's great

heart's courage even though his own
kin knew no mercy at his sword's edge.

The Scyldings' lady spoke:

"Empty this full cup my noble lord, my treasuregiver. Joy
be with you goldfriend of men & address these Geats with
the kind words they deserve, now let them know your thanks
for gifts that come to you from near & far. I've been told
you've asked this warrior to be a son to you. Bright Heorot,
hall of ringgifts, is cleansed so now make use of the gifts
you have to give & when fate's shaft strikes leave your kin
your kingdom & peoples. Hrothulf, I know, will still honor
these youths when you must depart this life, leave this earth.
Rest assured, Scyldings' friend, that he'll bestow favors
upon our sons when he remembers what glory & delight we
once brought his childhood."

Then turned
& walked along the bench to where

her sons sat with heroes' sons in
the company

of youth & there
between the brothers

sat Beowulf,
Geat & good man.

 FIT EIGHTEEN

FULL cup

        friendly words

woundgold

        goodwill

(Beowulf's)

          2 armbands (ornamented)
          robe & rings
          torc (earth's greatest)

There's no better heroes' hoard under clear skies,
none since Hama took the Brosings' gemset collar

      & fled for

        a bright city from

Eormenric's

      hate & craft

& entered

      eternity

a wise man.

115

That neckring the Great Hygelac,
Swerting's nephew, wore at his
last stand when by his blazon he
defended that treasure, guarded
slaughter's spoils & his pride
courted disaster: a feud with
the Frisians. That prince brought that jewel across high
                                    seas' waves & ended up slain
                                    under his shield. His body
                                    fell into Franks' hands
                                    along with his byrne & that
                                    ring. Warriors worse than
                                    he, however, escaped death to
                                    plunder those battle left
                                    hacked down. The field lay
                                    thick with dead Geats.
Noise: hall echoes.
Wealhtheow raised her hand before the company & spoke:

"Beloved Beowulf accept this torc, this robe,
our people's treasures. May they bring you
good luck & make you thrive.
                        By your might
prove yourself, teach these boys with mercy
& I will remember to reward you. Far & near
men will sing your praises forever wherever
seas skirt winds' cliffhomes.
                        May you flourish
for as long as you live. I wish you wealth,
riches, & treasure, noble warrior.
                        Joy is yours, may
your deeds make you my sons' friend. Here, these
gentle hearts, true to each other, swear allegiance,
united by loyalty & ready to serve.
                    Those who drink here do as I bid."

116

She took her seat. Then men resumed
their best of feasts & drank their wine.
None of them knew the fate grim destiny
set in store for a man laughing there.

Evening came.
　　　　　　　Hrothgar retired
to his chamber,
　　　　　　　the king took
to his bed.

Countless warriors remained in the hall
just as they used to,

benchplanks stripped, spread with
blankets, pillows & one of those

beerdrinkers, eager but doomed,
laid down on the hall floor.

Shields, boss & bright wood, above
their heads & there for all to see,

high helmets, ringed byrnes, great
wood shafts ready for battle always

ready, at home or in field, those
excellent folk stood by to answer,

at any hour, their lord's battlecry.

 FIT NINETEEN

THEY   slept

That night's rest cost
one man the raw, flat rate
common when Grendel held
that goldhall, before death
repaid him for his sinraids.

They all knew

something
outlived the Hellbeast,
survived the battlenight:

Grendel's mother
lumbered from her lair,
blood clouded her eyes.
The shebeast hurried to Heorot

where her son, shoot
      of Cain's seed, bud of
murdered brother's blood,
      shadowblossom of
browmark & swordedge

    escaped
        the Geat's grip
but not God's hand
      & came home to her
icy stream
      along death's road.

119

        Grendel's mother
burst in upon Danes,
                dead to the world,
sprawled all over their hall floor

as scrambled in sleep as the luck
        they woke to.

Shocked hands
           grabbed at swords,
shields
      over benches, above heads,
forgot
      byrnes, helmets

      Horror returned

struck not by woman

            not warrior

      The monster's mother
fumbled through lodgetangles,
             smashed
a thane, snatched her son's
          gory arm
in her frightened fist.

No blood crusted blades
hacked boar crests off helmets.

The confused shebeast fled,
ran for her swamps,

ripped limb in one hand,
the man asleep in the other,

killed by the creature's hug,
was brave Aeschere, Hrothgar's love.

When the gifts had been given
& the feast finished, the wine drunk,

Beowulf & his men went to spend
the night in digs of their own

beyond the uproar in Heorot
where both sides suffered

equal losses, equal gains:
pain's return, sorrow renewed.

The news of that thane,
dear to the gray king's heart,

brought the man grief.
he commanded his messenger:

"Bring me Beowulf!

When will God end our Hell?"

At crack of dawn

      floor boards thundered.

Battlelucky Beowulf

      & his men came up to,

into Heorot & crossed the hall

      up to wise Hrothgar:

"My lord,

      your night's sleep

was sweet, I trust.

            Has there

been any trouble here?"

Words caught

      in Hrothgar's throat,

Scyldings' helm answered:

 FIT TWENTY

"FORGET   all peace!
Grief returns to Danes.

Aeschere's dead.
What we shared:

            secrets stomping feet
            battles arms swinging

slashed boar emblems   blood
heads split wide open   noise
                         gone!

A bitch's bare hands crushed
that model man. Somewhere now
a beast's lips suck the bloody
stump of Yrmenlaf's brother

in revenge for that hard grip
of yours, the life torn from
that mother's son, that monster
who raided this hall & claimed
the lives of some of my best

warriors. I'm told two *things*
can be seen to prowl the nearby
borderlands, a male & female,
who dwell in swamps on"

123

"dark land

riddled with
wolfhills, windy

cliffs, risky
swamptrails where

upland streams

glimpsed
through cragfog

flow on
underground.

Not far,
a few miles from here,

a firmly rooted wood's
frost crusted branches

hand
shadows upon a lake

where each night sees
strange wonders:

firewaters,

flare above
unplumbed fathoms."

"Though the stag that stalks the heath

escapes the hounds through that wood,

he'd turn his antlers to the pack

to end their chase & bear their jaws

before he'd jump that bank.

Terror
keeps that spot.

Black water spouts
lift off the lake
& lap the clouds

Wind surges into
deadly storms until
all air grows dark.

The skies wail."

"Once again
I look to you
for help,

Beowulf.

You don't yet know
the terror
that lies upon
that land.

Track down
her lair,

return to
Heorot alive,

dare to
take on this feud

& rewards shall be yours:

gifts, goldbraids, old
treasures, my thanks."

FIT TWENTY-ONE

BEOWULF,

          Ecgtheow's son
weighed his words & said:

"Wise Hrothgar, do not grieve.

One day we will all die
so then let him who can

make his mark in this world
while he may:

fame, the dead warrior's
most prized possession.

Arise now, guardian of your kingdom.
Quickly, let us go
track down that woman.

I promise you
she will not lose us to
earth's bowels, mountain's woods
or ocean's depths,
wherever she may go!

Despite all that has happened,
be patient Hrothgar,
but then I expect no less of you."

The old king leapt up:

"Thank God for this man's words!"

	Hrothgar's
horse saddled,	braided mane
steer bridled,	wise, aged
ruler arrayed,	a large foot
troop readied.	

The parade of linden shields
marched in her tracks over

the clear cut ground trail
she hauled the corpse of

Hrothgar's dear housethane,
that best of youths, along

through woods onto moors.
That noble army pressed ahead

across steep rock slopes
on narrow paths singlefile,

on unknown roads, under precipice
& bluff, past many kraken haunts.

Hrothgar took a few of his wisemen & rode ahead
to size up the lay of the land when suddenly
they came upon a clump of mountain trees leaning
out over a gray rock. A murky wood. Bloody
water thick with gore stirred below them.

Pain wreaked
the hearts of
all Danes &
Scylding lords,

the grief of
many a thane
& all earls,

when they found
Aeschere's head
upon that cliff.

Those folk looked
down upon a
bloodwelled flood,
hot gore.

Time & again
the horn sung
an alarm, a
warsong.

The foot troops
all sat by that
water where

they saw hoards
of seadrakes,
krakens, explorers
of the deep,

stretched out
on slopes —
worms, wild beasts

who prowled
the sailroad
at midmorning.

129

When those bitter creatures heard

      that good horn's ring

they plunged enraged. A hard

      arrow flew from

the chief Geat's bow, hit its

      mark, slowed one's stroke

until death's wake overtook

      & swallowed him.

The water boiled with

      boar spears & sword barbs,

a fierce attack.

Men dragged the strange wave

roamer's dead hulk ashore &

gazed in wonder upon fathoms'

      ghostly guest.

Beowulf put on his gear, hero's armor.

He had no fear. His byrne, broad, handknit,
craftmarked, would explore those depths.

No grip of hate or war could crush the bones,
break the chest & grasp the life locked inside.

> & eddies made by the silver helmet
> that guarded his head
> would stir mud from
> the lake's bottom.
>
> The weaponsmith who shaped it
> bound it with bands
> & engraved it
>
> with swine images
> no battleblade could bite.

& he had a sword called Hrunting
lent him in his hour of need
by Hrothgar's spokesman, Unferth.

Peerless, ancient treasure,
not least of this hero's panoply.

Its steel edge, hard with bloodshed,
gleamed with a design: poison
twigs entwined. It failed no man

in battle or adventure
or wherever armies gathered.

Not a word of what
Ecglaf's son had said
when he was drunk
tempered the loan of
his sword to
the better warrior

He knew he
would never have
risked his life in
the surf.

He knew he
would have let
fame & glory go
then & there.

Not so
for the better man
once he
geared himself for war.

 FIT TWENTY-TWO

BEOWULF,

   Ecglaf's son,
turned to Hrothgar & said:

"Wise king, I'm ready to go now
but before I leave recall
that bond we share.

Famous son of Healfdene
& goldfriend of men,

should I lose my life
in your name will you be

my father when this world
is no more mine?

If battle claims me will
your hand guard my young men,

my closest friends?

& dear Hrothgar, the treasures
you gave me, will you send them

to the Geats' lord, Hygelac,
so that when he looks upon

that gold, Hrethel's son
will see & know I found

a good & wise ringgiver
& enjoyed his gifts while I could."

133

"I leave the sword
my fathers' fathers left me
to Unferth, man of wide renown,

       its ripple & waves
       its hard, cold edge
shall be his.
       Hrunting will earn me
my fame or death will take me."

       With those words
       without their replies,
       the Wedergeats' leader
       bravely departed.

    Surge, surf, billows
    waves swallowed the warrior.

The good part of a day passed
before he caught sight of level lakefloor.

At once that terrible mother of floods,
those deep regions' guardian for a hundred seasons,

sensed a man from above
entering her underwater otherworld.

She grabbed the warrior,
his sound body, his lithe limbs,
wrapped in knitrings, mail links,
safe from her horrible fingers' terrible grasp.

Swarms of
salamander seabeast snake
tusks tried
to break his sark as

lake shewolf
drug Beowulf

to the bottom
into her lair

helpless

hard as he tried
to swing his sword.

The warrior found himself inside
some enemy hall, safe from her waters,
out of her floods' sudden pull,
under a high ceiling, on dry land.

He saw a blink of firelight, bright
flash, its gleam lit the black cave.

The good man made out
                              the shape of
      that lakewife,
                  fathoms' hulk
& swung his warsword
      with all his might
                        wide unchecked.
The hard edge's coiled pattern hacked
her head, screamed its greedy warcry.

But the stranger's bright blade
had no bite, struck no quick.

135

His precious treasure failed him.

All those split helmets & doomed men's
slashed mail faded with its reputation
for the last & the first time.

     Hygelac's kin
never battleshy,
drew his breath. Glory
burned in his brain.

The angry warrior threw down his sword —
     engraved waves, wound wires, its hard
steel edge lay on the ground. He put all trust
     in his own fists' mighty force.

A man only does that when he means to win
the kind of fame which outlasts the battle
for without it his life adds up to nothing.

Rage blinded him. Without a second thought
the Wargeats' leader caught Grendel's mother
by the shoulder & knocked her to the floor.
As she fell she pulled him down, crushing him.
His head spun. She pinned him & reached for
her broad, burnished knife but no point or edge,
no mothers' revenge could pierce the mesh
that knit his breast's protection. Without its
hard but supple shell, without God's mercy,
the victory He held in the balance, Ecgtheow's son
would have lost his life beneath broad earth.

Once Beowulf was back on his feet
God's justice, the fight's outcome, was clear.

 FIT TWENTY-THREE

& THEN   he saw on her weapon heap

a sword
            charmed with luck,
a blade
            forged by ents,
an edge
            as sharp as wyverns' teeth.

The dream of all warriors gleamed
before him, the best of weapons,

too big for any man to carry into
battle's clash: good, well made,

giants' work.

            Scyldings' champion
grasped the chained hilt & drew
the patterned blade with hot but
grim heart. Without fear
for his life & with all his angry
might he struck a swordblow
that cracked her neck, shattered
its rings of bone & sliced clean
through her doomed heart.

            She slumped to the ground.

Sword's gore: warrior's joy.

137

Bright flash,
light burst forth

like sky's candle
as if that cavern
were clear heaven
at noon.

He stared around him at the room.
Hygelac's thane followed the wall
holding up his weapon firmly by
its hilt — cautious but brave:

Grendel's final payment
for all those raids he made on Danes,
the men he slew sleeping by Hrothgar's hearth,
those he ate & those he carried off.

The revenge of the 30 or so dead warriors
filled Beowulf's heart when he came upon
Grendel collapsed upon his bed, battle
worn, glazed & lifeless.

His corpse burst wide open when Beowulf
hacked off its ugly head.

Above whirlpools
of gore streams
of blood stained

the waters Hrothgar & his wisemen
had kept watch over the whole day.

Old, gray heads nodded:

"We've seen the last of him,
he'll not be back in all his glory
bringing our king a victory.

That seawolf's got him for sure!"

Day's ninth hour came.

Bold Scyldings broke camp, abandoned the slopes.

Good Hrothgar, men's goldfriend, turned homeward,

leaving his guests, that hero's crew, alone there.

Sick at heart they stared
out over the lake's murky waters,
hoping against all hope to see them part

& bear forth their friend & lord himself.

Then war's icicle dripped with ripe
hot gore, the iron edge's age
melted like chilblain ice in a blink

God's hand bends all things to its design:

summer's flux swarms winter's grasp
to season the hour & frost's crown turns
to floe's thaw & floods again.

Cold blood: dissolved blade.

Of all the treasures
      he saw in that trove
Wedergeats' leader
      took no more than

Grendel's head & that hilt

      set gems gleamed from,
whose blade engraved with braided waves
      hot gore burned up
& melted down with poisons from that

dead ghostbeast's body.

Return begun: he swam safe & sound
alive to see his slaughtered enemies,
& dove up through those waters whose

surge & waves now cleansed of
the morethanhuman who dwelt in them
when that ghostbeast lost his life:
his days: God's loan.

      With hard strokes
seafarers' captain came to land
      with laketreasures,
bearing the weight of their joy.

His crew ran to the shore to meet him,
thanking God to have their lord back alive
& well & quickly unbuckled his helmet & byrne.

      Peace upon the face of the waters
        beneath clouds
      pools of blood, slaughter's ripples.

They set forth with gladhearts
& retraced their own footsteps,
returning by way of old paths,
well marked straight tracks.

They came down off the lakeslopes
like a parade of kings,
carrying Grendel's head atop a spear.

No one of them could manage it alone.
4 strong men struggled with that burden.

               14 Geats, men of war
now came in sight of gold Heorot.
               A proud lord amid
his band crossed the meadhall's meadows.
               An earl's thane, a man
worth all his renown entered the hall.

Grendel's head
hauled by its hair across the floor:

men drinking dropped their cups,
earls & their queen gazed in terror
               upon this wonder.

❧ FIT TWENTY-FOUR ❧

BEOWULF,

            Ecgtheow's son,
greeted the Scyldings' leader,
Healfdene's son & said:

"Gladly we bring you
gifts from the lake,
victory's tokens,

                    spoils
of a close escape,

a hard fight almost lost
if God's shield hadn't
been there from the start.

Hrunting, a good blade indeed,
but there no more than useless steel,
failed me
        when Men's Guardian revealed
an old sword
           more than mansize
hung upon the wall & gave me time
to take it down. His mercy appears
when we need it most!

Two well placed strokes
at just the right times
brought down mother then son."

"& then

the broad battlesword's wavewoven blade
burned away in the blood that burst out,

the hottest gore any war ever shed.

Despite my enemies I've brought that hilt back:

vengeance was mine, fit payment for
their raids, the Danes left slaughtered
in their wake.

      Sleep, dear Hrothgar,
      free from worries
      about your warriors,
      men both seasoned & green.

      Sleep, Scyldings' prince,
      free from fear,
      your earls now lie
      safe beside your hearth."

& then

the old man's hand received that gold hilt,
thus the craft of ancient giants passed
unto the grayhaired lord, Denmark's greatest king.
A man who shared his wealth from sea to sea
now owned the treasure of God's enemies,
murderer & mother whose savage hearts
had long since ceased their beat.

Hrothgar gazed at the hilt,
that remnant of older days
engraved with their history:

CHAOS##FLOOD##OCEAN##GUSH
∫∫
GIANT##ONES##GONE##SURGE

They wore their web of fate
when they strayed from God
& drowned in His angry seas.

Runes on bright gold foils
named the man who had
that sword made, ordered its

hilt adorned with gleam
& twist of leaf & snake.

A hush fell. Hrothgar spoke:

"Let him who's upheld truth & justice,
whose past now floods his memory,
who's grown old guarding his homelands
say: This man was born to greatness!

Your fame, my friend will travel
all far roads & reach each nation.
Your heart rules your cool, wise hand.
I honor the promise, the bond we made.

Long life, Beowulf! Your nation's
comfort, your warriors' guardian
. . . unlike Heremod."

"Ecgwela's son grew up to be no joy to the Danes,
   instead he brought good Scyldings
death, slaughter & destruction.
   Often rage would overtake him
& he would attack his friends,
   the men who shared his board & battles
until he shunned them completely
   & shut himself off from their company.

This price God set above all men
   refused the Danes his treasures' honor.
In return, his joyless life
   brought him Hell's eternal misery.

   Let this be a lesson:
   Man's heart must be open.

   Listen well to what I tell you;
my wisdom comes from winters' ripeness.

It is a wonder the way God's strange design
grants some men wisdom, other land & rank
& how at times He allows a man his heart's desire,
giving him happy homelands here on earth,
a kingdom that stretches beyond his eyes,
a strongly manned fortress: all his to rule.

One day such a man will wake, look out his door
   & say: 'All this knows no end,
I am a rich man, age & sickness can't touch me.
Nothing casts a shadow on my long & happy life.
   No hate threatens what is mine.
The whole world goes my way, does my bidding.'"

♒ FIT TWENTY-FIVE ♒

"ALL   goes well,
too well,
pride takes root,
flourishes.

The soul's watchman
sleeps, too sound a
sleep, caught up in
days' cares.

The soulslayer
draws near unnoticed,
draws his bow, lets
go. An arrow

bites
the unguarded man's
heart. A shaft
poisoned with longing

pierces his soul.

That prince's days grow dark. His mind boils:

'I'm a selfmade man,
                    what's mine is mine alone.
Why should I share what little there's left?
I'm tired of my warriors,
                    that pack of thieves,
let'em cheat some fool who's got enough to share.'

147

"Thus he loses all of God's design
& death turns his body to dust in the wind.
Another inherits what was his
& without second thought, with open heart
bestows treasure where treasure is due.

Guard against this evil, dear
Beowulf, best of men, do what is
right & take its eternal reward.
Let no pride invade your mind,
renowned champion. Right now
& for awhile your strength is
at its height but soon enough
you will be stripped of that
glory by sickness or swordedge,

by fire's grasp,
by blade's bite,
by flood's surge,
by spear's flight
or oldage or
your eyes' clear light will dim & fade
& death overwhelm you.

Likewise, I ruled armored Danes a hundred
seasons under these skies, guarded them
in war with swordedge & spear from so many
of Midgarth's tribes that I too thought
no enemy beneath wide heaven could touch me.
& look how luck slipped through my hands,
how horror swallowed happiness when Grendel
made his way to my house & cast my mind
into misery with his unending raids. Praise
God Eternal Creator, I live to see this head
wet with gore, dripping like a warblade, &
an old feud's end!"

"Now take your seat.
Eat, drink to
your heart's content.

Your manifest glory
is our manifest joy."

Black night hooded
that hall of warriors.

They rose.
The old, gray Scylding longed
for his bed.

The Geat, mighty chieftain,
was glad for the chance of
a good night's rest.

& in those days they had
retainers in their halls
whose job it was to see
to all the needs of thanes
& traveling warriors &

one of these led Beowulf,

exhausted by his long journey
a long, hard adventure,

to bed.

The bighearted man rested
beneath a curved & gilded gablehorns,

inside the towering building
its guest slept

until the black raven
heralded by heaven's joy

& bright sunlight
buried away all shadows.

His warriors hurried, eager to get home.
The man whose heart had brought them
to that hall longed for the journey back,
to set out quickly for his ship, anchored
faraway.

Beowulf sent
Ecglaf's son his sword, steel Hrunting,
& thanked him for its loan
saying he thought it a good
& powerful battlefriend. The brave
warrior found that blade's edge blameless.

By then
his men were all ready & in their armor.

The noble leader whom the Danes esteemed
went to Hrothgar's highthrone.

The brave men saluted one another.

 FIT TWENTY-SIX

BEOWULF,

Ecgtheow's son said:

"We seafarers have come a long ways
& are eager to get back to Hygelac.

We have been treated well here,
what more could we wish for?

Lord of men, if there is ever
anything on earth that I can do
to win whatever love your heart
hasn't already shown me, tell me
        & I'll come at once.

If I get word across flood's vast stretch
that neighboring nations close in on you,
a threat you know well, then I'll bring
a thousand thanes & heroes to your rescue.
I know that Hygelac, however young, will
back me with word & deed, let me prove how
much I honor you with spearshaft & might.
When you need men most my aid will arrive.

    & if Hrethric, that prince's son,
      wants to come visit Geats' court
  let him come, he'll find friends there.

A good man should visit foreign lands."

& Hrothgar replied:

"It is God in you that speaks!

I've never heard a wiser, older man utter truer words.
Your hands may be strong but your heart is clear & ripe.

If spear, battle, sickness, or steel

should carry off Hrethel's son, your lord & folkshepherd,

then Seageats would never find

a better man than you to sit upon their throne & guard
their hoard if you were still alive & willing to rule

your kinsmen's kingdom.

The more I know you, Beowulf, the better I love you.

Your heart & mind please me.

All you've done here brings about a lasting peace between
Geats & Danes. The old inroads & fighting shall cease.

As long as I rule this wide land

our peoples shall exchange treasure,

our men greet each other with gifts:

across gannetwaters prow's curve will come with love's token.

Your race honors its treaties & feuds,
lives up to the old codes
with blameless lives."

Healfdene's son, heroes' shield,
gave Beowulf 12 more treasures
in that great hall
             & wished him godspeed,
a safe voyage home to his people.

The Scyldings' lord & noble king
kissed that best warrior, held
his face in his hands.

Tears in the old, gray man's eyes.

He wished without hope & knew
he would never see Beowulf again.

Grief flooded his heart,
his heartstrings held back a
dark longing
             that burned in his blood
for this dear man.

Beowulf left Heorot.

Gold treasures gleamed all about
the proud warrior as he walked

across grassy earth.

As they hurried along his men spoke
over & over about Hrothgar's gifts.

He was a peerless, flawless king
unto the end of his days when oldage

robbed him of his strength's joy &
brought him the ruin it brings many.

The seagoing craft

rode at anchor,

waited for

its lord & master,

its captain & crew.

154

HOMELANDS

being the second book of

BEOWULF

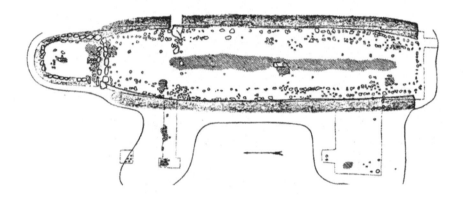

Homecoming

& then went down to sea,
ringnetted bodies, men in mailshirts, again that

      coastguard on hillbrow watched their return
      but this time rode down to greet them: new
      comers then, old friends now: those Weders.

      Broad seaship on sand. They loaded riches,
      trappings like spoils of war,

bore steeds aboard her, & over Hrothgar's hoard her
sturdy mast towered, &,

      Beowulf gave the man who guarded their boat
      a goldbound sword, an ancient heirloom that
      brought him men's honor when he returned to
      his place on the meadbench,

                        winds from sternward
bore their ship onward & away from Denmark
onto deep seas, her timbers thundered.
Wind jammed her, bellying sail's canvas, no waveswell
stayed her prow. They tossed into sight of Geats' cliffs,
hills that crew knew well, headlands along their shoreline.

The craft beached.
A man waiting then
watching for them
tied the ship up
to keep the undertow
from driving her back
onto waves' ebb & flow.

Beowulf ordered her cargo unloaded.

Not far from there
Hrethel's son, Hygelac,
lived in a lodge
with friends near
the edge of the sea
& with his wife, Hareth's daughter.

A clever, generous woman,
her gifts to Geats
were great indeed
although she spent
but a few short years
under that roof.

An altogether different queen
from Offa's wife Thryth.

Thryth

Dumb Offa,
prince thought a fool
who spoke at the ripe moment
& when asked why, replied:
There was nothing to say until now.

Brave Offa
whose stroke marked
the Eider as Angles' boundary
took Thryth to wive,
made her his queen.

She, a cousin of Charlemagne
cast to sea in a sailless craft
for wicked crimes,
came ashore off Ashland
& brought to

good Offa,
told a tale of trysts with churls,
wrapped him round her finger
with every woe
& her own great beauty til

noble Offa
named that banished woman Thryth
& married her.

None of his men
then dared to look on her,
even by day.

Such whims
become no queen
however beautiful.

Wise Offa,
they say on alebenches,
changed all that,
tamed the shrew
& won her love's respect.
So much so,
some thought her father
sent her cross greygreen waters
to seek out

proud Offa
who ruled his homelands well,
honored by all.
His son by her,
Eomer, Hemming's kinsman,
Garmund's grandson,
followed in his father's footsteps
as heroes' comfort & skilled fighter.

But then I've also heard
tales of how Thryth
plotted to overthrow
Mercia & its

first Offa
& killed Aethelberht,
her third daughter's suitor,
& died a violent death
herself soon after.

To card such a tangle
is no poet's job.

A good story is
a good story.

wide benches,
                    seameadows
glitter of sunrays,
                    homelands

15 men hurried to the hall
where word of their landing
drew crowds around a king
from oversea.

When they'd settled down
& Hareth's daughter
had passed the alecup,
Hygelac asked:

Well, Beowulf, what happened?
Did you calm Hrothgar's storm?
I've worried about you,
the way you just up & left us,
ran off for Heorot.

I still think
the Danes' troubles are
the Danes' troubles,
not ours.

But I'm glad
to see you home,
safe & sound.

Beowulf then told
Hygelac & the gathered company
the tale of Hrothgar's court,
his adventure oversea.

In passing he mentioned
the Scylding's daughter, Freawaru,
who sometimes passed the cup
at Heorot:

Hrothgar betrothed her to Ingeld
thinking this woman would settle
the slaughter so many feuds wrought

but after a prince falls
use soon cleans rust off swords
no matter how noble the bride may be.

The flower of Danish youth
armed with what was once Bards'
warriors seated their benches

& Freawaru bearing mead
could never be more than
a lingering memory of old wars

as long as Bards
still wielded blades.

& often an old spearman
would lean over & speak
to her betrothed:

Ingeld, the vines that entwine that blade there,
don't they mark the sword your father bore
into the war with the Danes? That iron, stolen from him
as he bled, hacked down on slaughter's field,
now arms some Scylding's son who treads
your enemy's hall with tales of murder on his lips.
You drink from a cup passed by your father's slayers.

Over & over the old man whispered bitter words
into Ingeld's ear until murder's blood stained
the bed of one of Freawaru's household.

The prince fled.
His love of Hrothgar's daughter died.
Peace between Danes & Bards faded.

When he finished his tale,
Beowulf presented Hygelac
with the boar standard,
helmet & byrne Hrothgar gave him,
as well as the 4 apple red horses.

The Bronsings' torc
went to Hygd along with
3 fine steeds.

A noble kinsman holds
nothing back from his lord.

Hygelac's nephew was a good man.
Never did he slay his fellow warriors
in drunken brawls.
Yet his gentle heart
was capable of great anger in battle.

A noble warrior now,
he was once thought a fool.

The Bear's Son

One spring night a warrior & his wife were
wakened from sleep by a loud noise & fierce
growls outside their window. The warrior
went to investigate, thinking some wild beast
was attacking his horses. When he returned
his bed was empty, his wife gone.

Late the next night, after searching all that
day, the warrior found his wife in a clearing
near a bear den by a heap of ashes where a
fire had been. She was bruised & dazed,
muttering of some black beast like a bear that
had carried her there. The warrior brought
his wife home.

An old leech attended her, administering
feverfue to ease her spasm, periwinkle to
drive away the fear & beewort to discharge
the poisons she felt in her womb.

She grew strong again. The dreams that troubled
her soon faded although she often woke at night,
saying she heard loud groans & saw the room
lit by fire's light.

Late that winter she bore a third son for
her husband.

As the boy grew he became duller & duller,
unable to speak. He seemed a fool.
Often the child wandered into the woods
to return covered with beestings, licking
honey from his dumb lips. For that reason
his brothers called him little Beewolf,
Honey Hunter.

Years later, a neighboring king sent word
that some great beast raided his lodge each
night & killed his best men. Being a good
man, the warrior sent his own sons to aid
the king. The youngest, Beewolf, went
along to help carry their weapons & watch
their horses.

On Yule eve the two brothers, left alone
in the great hall, waited for the monster
to appear. He came. They surprised him
but hard as they fought neither was a match
for the beast's strength. Yet both
brothers did escape with their lives.

Beewolf waited outside in the snow with
the horses & saw the beast flee the hall
fight. He followed his fresh tracks
into the wood where the creature disappeared
down a dark hole. Beewolf entered the
earthcave after it. Inside he caught sight
of a cold, icy glowing blade which he took
from the wall & used to slay the monster.

The next morning he returned again to the lodge
dragging the beast's bloody head. He
presented the king with the ancient sword.
None of the warriors could believe what
they saw. The king then rewarded Beewolf
with many treasures.

As the brothers rode home again laden
with gifts, they spoke of Beewolf's
great deed & saw that he was no longer
a boy or fool. He was now a proud &
able warrior, their better by far.

From that day forth until his death,
Beewolf spoke, not like a common warrior
but like a king with wisdom & from a
clear ripe heart.

Then Hygelac had
Hrethel's goldtrimmed heirloom fetched.
Geats had no greater treasure.

He laid that blade
in Beowulf's lap
& gave him 7000 hides
of land, a hall & a throne.

Both now had
bloodrights to landshares
in that country,
an inheritance to leave sons,
the greater span of which,
that broad kingdom itself,
belonged, by right,
to the man higher in rank.

Oldage

50 winters
        his homelands' guardian
seed of
        his destruction,
daylight failed
        in the garden of his years

& it came to pass in later days
that battle's clash no longer rang in Hygelac's ears.
He lay upon the field, deaf to all life's sounds.

Not long after, his son Heardred
fell to his death beneath the shelter of his shield,
singled out by the Scylfings as targets of their hate.

& so it came about that Geats' broad kingdom
fell into Beowulf's hands to rule wisely & well.

Then one night
a man stumbled into
a secret tunnel that ran
beneath a rock barrow
near the sea, on Geats'
coastline.

Its narrow passage
led straight
to the heart
of a lost hoard

whose guardian slept
but not for long.

Crawling along the shaft
the man soon found
that it opened out
into a chamber piled high
with a heathen hoard.

Just as he spotted
the riches' sleeping keeper,
his eye fastened upon something
shining within his grasp.

His hand itched
to reach & hold the thing.
He plucked it from the heap
& ran
back along the tunnel til
his nostrils filled
with night air
& seawind soothed
his sweaty brow.

The man who broke into that barrow
& sowed ruin's seed
did so out of no design,
no need, no meadhall boast.

Pure accident, mere chance
brought him to
that long forgotten earth door.

He was some warrior or other's
slave running away from a flogging
looking for a place to hide.

But once inside,
his blood tingled,
his bones chilled.

A confused, unhappy victim
of lust caught by the sight
of something glittering
beyond his wildest dreams.

That earth house held
a wealth of just such precious,
ancient riches cunningly
hidden there by a sole survivor
of a noble race.

That lone man,
his name now lost, knew
his days were numbered,
the time left to enjoy
what took his tribe
generations to hoard
all too brief.

With grief he built
a barrow to guard
his kinsmen's hoard
for ages to come.

fresh dirt,
        grassless rocks

On the headlands,
on flat, open ground,
by the sea,
a newly dug mound stood open,
ready to be sealed with runes
& filled with a heritage
worth hoarding, fighting for,
hiding.

Before it
a man keened:

The hard helmet emblem cracks.
The boy to shine it sleeps.

No hawk swoops to glove.
No horse stamps in garth.

The harp's sound
faded from his hall forever,
silenced by
clash of shields,
slash of steel.

Mail crumbled.
Byrnes came to rest.

The lone man
asked earth to guard
what warriors could not,
the wealth they'd won
from it.

He closed the barrow
& wandered
til death overtook
his heart.

naked snake,
          mound hunter,
night flyer,
          ribbon of fire

A primeval beast,
a haunter of dawn's halflight,
discovered the earth door
wide open, its stones
fallen away.

Inside, the dragon
grew old, wallowing
in pagan gold
300 winters.

His earth encrusted hide
remained as evil
as ever, unchanged
by dream or time or gold.

A simple cup,
never missed.

Please master,
don't beat me.
I've got a gift.
I found it underground.
I'll be good.

Hoard ransacked,
loss noticed.

Go.
Fancy that,
a fool finding
this.

manstink,
       footprints

The worm woke
sniffed the air
& slithered out
along the rocks

looking for
traces of sleep's
intruder & found
his track,

a trail that led
over wasteland.

In the web of things
God spared that fool,
let him go unharmed.

The Lord's plan
allowed the man
time to escape &
time to rouse

a wrath that would
mark another's death.

The dragon then discovered
the theft, noticed a loss,
something missing,
a gold cup.

Battle thoughts
swarmed his black heart.
It flickered
with a rage bound in joy.

300 winters' ice
melted into hot fury.
All neighboring nations
would rock with its flood.

The snake could hardly wait
for night to trade
his fire for the cup's theft.

○ THOMAS MEYER

a dark moon
        sat on

Geats' headlands

Day faded. The rage
that swelled inside
the barrow keeper's
coils burst forth.

A shower of flame
lit night's black skies.

Earthdweller's terror
like lightning before
thunder heralded the end
of a good king's reign.

hot coals
            rained,
houses
            blazed,
all air
            burned.

Men shuddered. Women
& children ran from their beds.
Midnight flashed with
a horrible noon.

Daybreak
& a fire ring
held Geats inside
a flame cup of
death & destruction.

Firstlight
& the dragon fled
for his hoard,
mound walls' safety
& his battlestrength's protection

not knowing
the ruin he'd spun
with his own as well.

Word of that disaster
spread quickly to
Geats' distant borders
where Beowulf had gone
to inspect his broad
kingdom's farthest reaches.

He learned how
his own home, hall
& throne was
a pile of ashes now.

The source
of all Geats' gifts
& reward lay buried
beneath charred rubble.

Pain filled his heart,
trouble his mind.

Where had he gone wrong?
What ancient law went unheeded?
God's revenge must have a reason.

Beowulf was not a man to cry out:
Lord, why me? He accepted his lot,
tried to change the bad, enjoy the good.

Never had a catastrophe disturbed him so.

Second thoughts invaded his mind.
A kind of doom flooded
the chambers of his heart.

He returned to find
his land's coastline destroyed.
Dragonfire left his fortress
& stronghold ruins.

Revenge was the only answer.

Geats' lord ordered
an iron shield forged for him.
No wood, not even linden,
could withstand the heart
of the battle looming before him.

Out of the midst of the fire,
of the cloud & of the thick darkness

a tale of theft came to darken
the old king's heart.

Geat's lord chose
11 men to go with him
to the worm's lair.

But he alone would do battle there.

The thief, ruin's instrument,
was that party's 13th member,
their guide. He led them
toward the sea.

As he neared the barrow & heard
waves crash upon rocks, he trembled.

His pitiful mind shined
with memories of woundgold hidden
by rock & dirt, guarded
by a beast that filled his weak heart
with terror.

The sound of the band's approach
woke the threat to the treasure
the king's body guarded, his soul.

Soon it would shed
its flesh coat.
The snake stirred
from sleep.

Geats' goldfriend came to the headlands,
halted, turned to bid his men
farewell.

Beneath earth
death woke.

He stared at the young warriors' faces,
recalled how at 7 years
he'd been brought to Hrethel's court,
clothed & fed by a good lord
who loved him
as much as he loved his own heirs,

Hygelac & his brothers,
Herebald & Hothcyn.

A shadow lurked
back of the old king's mind,
a grief tipped dart.

Herebald & Hothcyn

2 young brothers stood
with bow & arrow in the yard,
sharpening their aim.

Hothcyn's turn. He drew
the horn inlaid bow's string,
let go. His hand slipped.

The arrow shot, found its mark
deep inside Herebald's heart.

It is written:
Such a murder must go unrevenged,
no blood money collected
for brother killing brother.

Yet such laws can't ease
a father's loss.

Hrethel's loss
echoed that of the old man
whose young son swung
from gallows as
crow's carrion.

His grief
matched that of the old father's song:

Dawn brings me nothing
but memories.

My son's horsemen sleep,
earth hides his warriors.

His house a shell.
Only wind walks there.

Alone I lie in my bed & keen,
my fields all too wide now.

The same sorrow
swarmed Hrethel's heart.

Left helpless
by lack of revenge,
that king departed men's
earthly company
to bask in God's
heavenly light

& left his sons
wide lands, great riches.

HOTHcyn
HOTHr

———————————————

BALDr
HereBALD

That rime
recalls Aesir's grief.

Sometimes
mute fate leaves
signs upon our lips,
in our ears.

Beowulf's sad heart
shook with rage, ready for
slaughter as he spoke,

his end drew near:

Look for no Dane, Swede or Gifthas
to lead your armies as long as Beowulf lives.

When battle calls I'll be there.

This hand & the hard blade it holds
are ready to fight for the hoard.
Let earth part & the worm come forth.

I'd cast aside my sword, helmet & byrne
& take him on barehanded like I did Grendel.

But I think this fight, marked by fate,
will be fought with fire's hot edge.

Enough of an old man's bragging.
I'm ready to begin this battle.

God, let its outcome be quick.
I want victory or death,

that gold or my own swift end.

He adjusted his helmet,
took up his shield

& walked to the foot
of that rocky cliff.

His mail clanked.

A great river
gushed up from under
vast stone arches.

A fire flood
burst out of the barrow's dark depths.

Bathed in flame,
the warrior's breast heaved.

A stream of battlewords
roared down the cave,
rang beneath the wide skies,
echoed off rocks:

Come,
shake off sleep.

A sharp sword awaits you,
worm.

manspeech
        struck dragonears,
maelstrom,
        dim, smoky air
heavy with
        war's stink

Beowulf lifted his sword.

Engraved leaf's glint.
Blade slash. Coil,
uncoil, recoil.

Fate's spiral tightened.

That ancient heirloom
didn't have the bite
the old king counted on.

That warrior stood
in the midst of a battle
that allowed him no victory.

His good sword struck bone,
stopped dead.

Fire belched.
Farflyer's anger.
A warrior's blow.

The dragon got his breath back.
War lit the skies. Flames licked
at the man who'd once ruled his race.

Ecgtheow's son would soon
abandon his house on earth
for another elsewhere.

Geats' flower
of manhood hurries
home to mother's lap,
its king left
on hot coals.

Why did you ever
leave your hearth?
There the women
need you to blow
the ashes like girls.

What about pledges, the services
you said you'd render for shields & swords?

I, for one
won't come home
til the worm's dead.

Side by side,
my lord & I
will end this feud.

Weders turn coward.
The land we save's
no longer worth it.

Nothing shakes loose
the kinship bonds
that fetter a good
man's heart.

The whole tribe
thrives on
its king's body.

No fear held Wiglaf back.
He gripped his yellow linden shield,
drew his old sword,
heart & mind steady as a rock.

The first battle he fought
arm to arm with his lord
loomed before this hero.

When he looked upon
his king circled in flame,
pain flooded his heart with debt.

He recalled the old man's gifts:
the Waegmundings' homestead &
a rightful share of his father's
commonlands.

✦ THOMAS MEYER

Inside that furnace,
he choked on poison smoke,
called out to Beowulf:

Fight on,
defend your honor.

I'm here
to protect a man
who risks his life
for his land's sake.

Wiglaf's raised shield
went up in flames.

He dropped it & sought
cover behind his kinsman's.

The glow from
a red hot boss on the ground

lit the barrow's
thick air.

Beowulf attacked.
His sword fell
with all the glory
that burned in his brain.

Naegling
struck the worm's head
& halfway in
split in two.

The broken blade
cast a long shadow
upon the king's field.

No manmade weapon
could withstand
the shock of his stroke.

That warrior
put no trust in
the blades he carried
to battle, however hard.

The firedrake, Geats' plague,
lay stunned then regained his breath,
charged again, the third time.

His jaw, a knife wreath, clamped
upon Beowulf's neck.

The warrior wore a bloody torc
of dragonteeth.

Then & there
Wiglaf won
his birthright.

He ignored his burning wounds
& jabbed his bright sword
into a spot lower down on the worm.

○ THOMAS MEYER

snakefire
   flickered
died down,
   faded little
by little

The grayhaired man's head cleared.
He drew the deadly knife tucked inside his byrne.

With one stroke
the dragon's soft, hot, bloated underbelly

ripped open. Live coals showered
the kinsmen's victory.

ruin's
    rune

Beowulf's wound,

that king's last great deed,
earth's last great victory,

the land we save's no longer worth it.

Black poisons flooded
the chambers of the old Geat's heart.

He stumbled as far as wall's ledge,
sunk down there lost to pain.
The curve of those entbuilt arches,
the barrow roof held up by rock,
filled the vault of his brain

with dark memories of a great race
drowned by flood.

His eyes' light faded slightly.

A cool breeze
from up off the sea
blew through the barrow.

Wiglaf,
blood spattered, battle weary,
fetched fresh stream water
to wash his lord's wounds.

Beowulf spoke,
hardly able to speak,
his limbs & mind feverish with pain,
the last day of his days on Midgarth
pressed in on him:

```
                   my wargear
my  son   if one   outlived me
to   give   to

50 winters  a  good  king  un
attacked      safeland    open
heart   the pain  God   takes
my   unstained by    kinblood

go   hoard    grayrock worm
dead   bring me   gold  gems

ease pain   let  me  die    look
ing on     them    go
```

His lifebreath regained,
Weohstan's son ran
to obey his dying lord.

Farther down,
under barrow arches,
his hard, handlinked
byrne rang,

echoed along the ledge.
Walls sparkled with the gem glow,
gold glint.

A man may hide his hoard underground
but O how greed's itch can overtake
the hands that reach for such riches.

In the worm's lair,
den of that creature that flew
through dawn's halflight,

he found
cups left unshined
ages upon ages & emblems
rusted off helmets.

& atop the pile
he caught sight
of a goldwound blazon staff
from which light flashed.

Blaze filled air
lit the cavefloor.

Wiglaf gazed
upon past ages' craft

yet saw no trace
of its guardian,
asleep or awake.

Death now sealed the worm
in God's Helldream.

There in a thief's shadow,
a Waegmunding plundered the ancient
network, loaded his arms

with cups, rings, gems
& that bright, emblem gleaming staff.
He hauled all he could carry

back to his lord quickly
for fear he'd find him dead
where he left him.

He dropped the riches at Beowulf's feet,
fetched another helmet full of water
& washed the old man's bloody face.

The grayhaired Geat's grief filled mind
came to, words as clear as spring water
broke through his heart's throb:

Now that I die & my days on earth end,
I want to thank Almighty God for the gifts
you set before me. Wiglaf, my throne
is yours, you must answer Geats' needs,
this hoard has cost them their king.

Out on headlands, by the sea, build a mound
where my pyre burned, so sailors upon the flood
can chart their course through seamist's cloud by
a landmarked towering high above Whale Ness
called Beowulf's Barrow.

Take my torc, armband, byrne & helmet.
They're all worthless to me, make good use of them.
You, last of Waegmundings' blood,
must protect our kin's glory. Death,
as fate decreed, bears me away.

Soon hot fires would destroy
the old man's noble flesh,
his soul go unto God's keeping.

His last words faded
as Wiglaf stared upon the pitiful,
charred body of his lord.

Near it lay the coils
of that earthsnake whose loathed shaped
would never whirr through dead of night

again. All this almost more
than he could bear.

He walked out of the dark
into light.

fresh air
      heavy with salt

10 men came
from the wood
filled with shame.

Wiglaf took up a helmet
of water, turned his back to them,
returned to his lord, the man
they'd failed to defend
in his hour of need.

He'd no words
for those weaklings, mock
warriors. There'd be
no more gifts, swords,
landshares, homesteads for
them. They & their kin
outcasts set to wander
a life not worth living.

No water
roused Beowulf now.

A rider rode
down to the barrow
from the cliff edge
where warriors camped
awaiting word of
their lord's return or death.

He looked on
his king's corpse
& the gashed body of
his enemy & Wiglaf
crouched beside
them both.

& sped back to the men
with this news.

That messenger
left nothing unsaid:

Geats' lord, the man
who granted us
all our desires, lies
on slaughter's bed
near the worm
he overcame, the hoard
he won & his own
broken blade.

Weohstan's son
sits at his side,
the living keeping
watch over the dead:

one loved, one loathed.

We must prepare for war at once.

News of our king's fall
will soon reach
both Frisians & Franks.
& when Swedes
hear of our sorrow
their minds will fill
with memories
of Ravenswood
& the battle fought there.

Quick now,
let's go look on
our chief,
bear our ringgiver's corpse
to his pyre.

More than
one man's share
of hoard gold will melt
away in fires
that lap up that brave warrior.

An untold wealth.
A hard, grim bargain.

Beowulf paid
for those rings,
final goal of his life,
with his last breath.

All that
flame, blaze will
swallow, devour.

None of it will
gleam, a keepsake
upon some brave man's arm,
round some bright maid's neck

& she'll wander
world's end, sad hearted,
stripped of gold,
not once
but over & over
again until
her feet ache, her breasts burst

now that her leader's
laid aside
hall's laughter, mead's joy.

Many a cold spear
grasped at gray dawn
will lift in morning air.

It won't be
harp's sweet strum
that wakes warriors from sleep.

The greedy raven will have tales
to tell the eagle of feats shared
with the wolf on slaughter's field.

A great silence
entered the hearts
of all gathered there.

That messenger
left nothing unsaid.

They all rose,
walked down to
the foot of Eagle Ness,

saw through
their tears
an ineffable wonder.

Nothing troubled
their lord & ringgiver's dreams.

He didn't stir from
his sleep on those sands.

But before they beheld
that peace, the quiet
that bound their hearts
with strength to face
forthcoming battles &
earth's eventual ruin,

their eyes caught sight of
the hateful snake,

the fire dragon's
coils stretched out on the ground,

a coalblack rainbow 50 feet long.

He'd tread air's dark kingdom no more.
Earth's eternal shelter held him fast.

Cups, plates,
gold dishes, swords

rusted, corroded
by a 1000 winters' rest
in earth's deep breast.

Shining heritage
of men & ents of old
bound with a spell
only a God chosen
man could break.

The Lord Himself
Glory's King & Men's Shelter,
grants each man the fate
that fits him best.
That treasurehall
was Beowulf's lot,
his good life's end.

The beast,
guardian of the hoard hidden there,
got nothing from that battle
but death.

The dragon
slew one man,
only one,
all the blood needed
to work out fate's plan.

The scene of a warrior's
last stand remains
a mystery. He never knows
if after the battle
he'll sit drinking mead
with friends again.

So it was with Beowulf,
death made that mission his last.

Charms
knitted from dark runes,

black strokes
sealed that hoard:

He who breaks this circle we weave
unleashes ruin upon Midgarth.

All Mankind will fall as sin's
prisoners in false gods' groves,

bound tight in Hell's eternal chains.
Only earth's end will lift this plague.

Wiglaf spoke:

Often many must endure
the sorrow one man works.
So it is with us.
Nothing we could have said
would have kept our lord
from this deed.

I've seen treasure,
saw it once death cleared the way,
brought down the mound's rock walls.

& so has Beowulf & in his grief,
in the face of the gold of his undoing,
despite the pain, the old man
told me to bid you farewell
& ordered us to build him
a barrow high above his pyreplace.

& so we shall. In what little
time's left mankind, it'll become
as renowned among nations
as he was in life.

7 of you follow me,
we'll inspect the hoard's remains.
The rest of you
pile up a great bier by the sea
so that when we return
we can carry our king's body
to its final home, deliver him
unto God's arms.

Gather timbers for dark fires,
for the blaze that will leave
our chief embers, ashes of
a great fighter who'd endured
many arrows' rain when bowstrings
sent feathershafts over shieldwalls,
who'd outlived many battlestorms.

Weohstan's son
that band's 8th man,
lifted a torch,
led his chosen men
by its light to the gold.

There they drew
no lots to share out
what gleamed before them

but carried it all
in silence to the barrow's mouth.

Then shoved the worm's hulk
over the cliff. Waves received
an ancient gift, rings' & riches'
keeper.

The 8 men loaded a wagon
with woundgold & brought
that great wealth &
their grayhaired warchief
to Whale Ness.

& the Geats built there a pyre
piled high with helmets, shields,
bright byrnes & spears.

Aloft they laid their dead lord
then kindled that great blaze.

Flames & weeping rose
high above seacliffs.

Wind died down as fire broke
the king's bone fortress, swarmed
his heart.

Grief filled all Geats.

A woman keened:

Sorrow binds my hair.
I outlive my lord.

Days of mourning,
months of slaughter,

seasons of terror
imprison my people.

Helpless we fall.
All Midgarth rots.

He set out now
in smoke upon the sea.

It took Weders
10 days to build
Beowulf's Barrow
raising walls & roof
round & over
what the fires left.

Inside the mound
designed by wisemen
they laid armrings,
gems, trappings
taken from the long lost hoard.

They left earth
to guard the gold
where to this day
it still lies fast
underground, safe
from men's hands & eyes.

○ Thomas Meyer

12 brave men
rode round the mound
& spoke,
each in turn,
their praise of their lord:

It is very meet, right & our bounden duty —
gentle, gracious, kind king.

& then went on their way

APPENDIX A

Interview with Thomas Meyer[1]

DH: You've mentioned that for your senior thesis at Bard during the 1970s, you decided to translate "three quarters of the extant poetry in Old English, including *Beowulf*." How long did that take you? I realize it's relatively small, but still, I'd imagine, a considerable amount of work. What was your training in Anglo-Saxon prior to taking that on — did it mostly come at Bard?

TM: Despite the translations I've done and some of my earlier work, I'm really an academic or scholar manqué. So what was meant by my statement about that 1969 senior project was that apart from *Beowulf* (not "including" it), i.e., what's left then, my work covered "three quarters of the extant poetry in Old English." Having just checked Wikipedia, can't give you the line count, which was how that figure came about. Anyway, you're right, it's not a huge amount.

Otherwise, I had no training in Anglo-Saxon. The faculty had approved me for doing a creative project, a bunch of poems. But in his wisdom Robert Kelly took me aside and said, "Look, you're going to write the poems anyway, why not use this opportunity to learn something you might not otherwise?" I'd had a Chaucer course and eventually did a paper on "The Franklin's Tale," all of which fascinated me. Old English seemed like the natural next step and there was a faculty member who was willing to be my advisor and

---

[1] This interview was conducted by David Hadbawnik in Autumn 2011.

tutor me. The romance that held me was being in on the ground floor of English. Otto Jesperson's *Modern English Grammar on Historical Principles* (1909-1949) had provided a lot of treasure in that direction.

DH: Next, you talk about translating — at Gerrit Lansing's suggestion — Cockayne's "Leechdoms, wortcunning, and starcraft of early England" (and wound up also doing Apuleius's *Herbarium*). What (besides Gerrit) drew you to this, and what kind of different challenges did this translation present compared to something like *Beowulf*?

TM: I was living with Jonathan Williams in the Yorkshire Dales, in the countryside, and the plant matter was pretty much right there under my feet. And the *Herbarium* had a certain occult edge to it I liked, obviously, plus an element of British folklore that got appended during the rendering of the Latin original into Anglo-Saxon.

Anyone who takes even the slightest glance at Old English can see the huge difference between the language of its prose and the language of its poetry — that's probably the ground of my interest and attraction to the material in the first place. My idea about translating the *Herbarium* was to keep the language, syntax, and vocabulary as simple as possible, as "native," avoiding all Latinate forms.

DH: Basil Bunting, you've said, was a "frequent visitor and table companion" during the time you were working on Old English. Obviously, his *Briggflatts* engages with Anglo-Saxon as well.[2] Or perhaps not so obviously; at any rate, Chris Jones, in *Strange Likeness*, his study of 20th-century poets and Old English, writes, "the influence of Old English in [Bunting's] own poetry seems to me

---

[2] Basil Bunting, *Briggflatts: An Autobiography* (1965; Tarset, UK: Bloodaxe Books, 2009).

impossible to separate from that of Old Norse."[3] He quotes Bunting saying, "I think our best hope of an art or literature of our own does not lie in imitating what has come to us from Rome or Europe or from the South of England, but in trying to discern what is our own, and to develop it and fit it for 20th- and 21st-century conditions." The two of you discussed the "long poem," and I'm curious to what extent those conversations helped shape the direction you went in with your *Beowulf* translation.

TM: How can someone mid-twentieth century . . . . Wait, is it even possible to create a kind of rhetorical equivalent in modern English of Old English poetic diction without slipping into some sort of pre-Raphaelite, William Morris affectation? Bunting thought Coverdale's and Tyndale's translations of the Bible was the place to look; that the King James Version watered down their strengths. Well, as the above quote about "the best hope" makes clear, the bias was Northern.

Linguistically his essential interest was Welsh, and to some extent Norse, elaborate verse forms, the sort of thing English, even Old English, can't quite do, not having enough curly-cues, inflected formations, and pure rhyme. *The Book of Kells* he would point to as a visual representation of what he was after aurally.

Because of these discussions, translating *Beowulf* suddenly stared me square in the face. Something of a mess as far as "long poem" is concerned, but a real gymnasium for trying out the possibilities of a poetic language. That was my real concern. The natural source for grand eloquence in contemporary English, it then seemed to me, was Elizabethan, the Bible. Not Shakespeare, who has always struck me as too clever by half, as they say, and just too, too much in general, in spite of all his "humanism."

---

[3] Chris Jones, *Strange Likeness: The Use of Old English in Twentieth-Century Poetry* (Oxford: Oxford University Press, 2006), 13.

To be fair, Bunting's major point was not the lack of a poetic diction in contemporary English, but that "the long poem" was no longer a possibility because of the speed at which the culture changes. He used to point out that he paid the same rent for a room near the British Museum that Charles Dickens had a hundred years previously. That cultural stability vanished by 1914. Since then, eventually the only long poem possible he thought was autobiographical. [Louis] Zukofsky's *A*, or [his own] *Briggflatts*.[4]

DH: I think I'm most intrigued with your statement that, "instead of the text's orality, perhaps perversely I went for the visual. Deciding to use page layout (recto/verso) as a unit. Every translation I'd read felt impenetrable to me with its block after block of nearly uniform lines. Among other quirky decisions made in order to open up the text, the project wound up being a kind of typological specimen book for long American poems extant circa 1965." I wonder if you could talk more about that — were there any translations in particular you'd seen that bothered you (or any since then)? Any books in particular that influenced your visual structuring? I immediately thought of Dorn's *Gunslinger*.[5]

TM: There's not a translation of *Beowulf* that doesn't have me yawning. Having said that, Edwin Morgan's and Michael Alexander's are maybe my favorites. The Seamus Heaney strikes me as somehow pedestrian, at the same time somehow overbearing.[6]

DH: There seemed to be, at that time — say late 1960s, early 1970s — a lot of interest in Anglo Saxon poetry, perhaps responding to Pound's influence: [for example,] you, Michael Alexander, and Bill Griffiths, later to get a degree in Old English, who published a small

---

[4] Louis Zukofsky, *"A"* (Berkeley: University of California Press, 1978).

[5] Edward Dorn, *Gunslinger* (Durham: Duke University Press, 1989).

[6] See Edwin Morgan, *Beowulf: A Verse Translation into Modern English* (Aldington: Hand and Flower Press, 1952) and Seamus Heaney, *Beowulf: A New Verse Translation* (New York: W.W. Norton, 2001).

edition of a translation by John Porter in 1975.[7] We now know, too, of course, that Jack Spicer studied Old English with Arthur Brodeur at Berkeley, and did his own translation of *Beowulf*.[8] Meanwhile, Paul Blackburn had worked on medieval Spanish, translating *El Cid* in 1966.[9] I wonder to what extent you were conscious of there being some sort of medieval "revival" going on, and whether you talked (with Lansing or Bunting, say) about the potential such older forms might have for your poetry.

TM: I don't know, I felt completely isolated. This was a time of the Great American Presence in UK Poetry, and the creation of American Studies programs at new UK universities. Clearly Anglo-Saxon had fallen out of fashion in the early 1960s, dead and buried by 1970. When Michael Alexander's translation appeared in 1973, personally it came as a complete shock.

Nor did anyone mention Anglo-Saxon as an influence on me, apart from a kind of nerdiness. My own work at the time was definitely involved with "early Anglo-Saxon lore," plants, local legends, Englishness. What nineteenth-century vicars wrote diaries about, or someone up at the manor collected, birds' eggs, bezoars, or household tales. After all, that's where I was living. The English Countryside.

However, one of the most profound effects Anglo-Saxon had on me from the beginning and to this day, as I've said, is avoiding the Latinate.

---

[7] See Michael Alexander, *Beowulf: A Verse Translation* (1973; London: Penguin, 2001) and John Porter, *Beowulf: Anglo-Saxon Text with Modern English Parallel* (London: Pirate Press, 1975).

[8] See David Hadbawnik and Sean Reynolds, eds., *Jack Spicer's Beowulf, Parts I-II*, CUNY Poetics Documents Initiative, Series 2.5 (Spring 2011).

[9] See Paul Blackburn, *A Poem of the Cid: A Modern Translation with Notes*, ed. George Economou (1966; Norman: University of Oklahoma Press, 1998).

DH: Perhaps along those same lines, how important was the influence of Pound — obviously there in the case of Bunting, but what about "next generation" poets like yourself in approaching Anglo Saxon material?

TM: [Ezra] Pound was The Influence. His "Seafarer." Because of it I decided on Old English for the Bard Senior Project. As a translator (Old English, Chinese, Greek, Sanskrit) he's my model, in particular "Homage to Sextus Propertius." Me, I'm not a "real" translator, someone working hard to be faithful to the original text, at the same time writing good, clear English. That I admire. Immensely. My excuse for bending and re-shaping the original text, often straying from it radically, is that mine are not the only available translations in English. They weigh heavily on the pan of the scales marked "commentary," as in "all translation is commentary," each choice a nudging of the text in a certain direction.

DH: Turning to the translation itself: Right away, you seem to signal that this is going to be quite different than other verse translations. Here is Jack Spicer's version:

> Hwæt, We Gardena   in geardagum,
> Lo, we ~~of the spear Danes~~ in former days
> Lo, we ~~of the spear Danes~~ have heard
>
> þeodcyninga   þrym gefrunon,
> of the kings of the people glory have heard
>   *of the spear Danes*
>
> of the glory^ of the kings of the people in former days,
>
> hu ða æþelingas   ellen fremedon!
> how the princes (deeds of) valor performed.
> how the princes performed deeds of valor.

With the second line of text being his rough draft, the third the version he ultimately decided on. Even that first word, "Hwæt," is notoriously difficult to render; Seamus Heaney has it, "So." Others have used "Listen," etc. Then you are presented with the syntactical difficulties, as is apparent from Spicer's obvious struggles to figure out what to do with the genitive plural "Gardena."

At any rate, here's yours:

> HEY   now hear
>
> >> what spears of Danes
> > in days of years gone
> > > by did, what deeds made
> > their power their glory —
>
> > their kings & princes:

The "HEY   now hear" seems both an obvious and radical solution, as it hints at a sonic relationship to "Hwæt" while being pretty informal, like someone getting people's attention at a party. You don't bother trying to approximate the syntax, or indeed worrying about the overwhelming genitives — for that matter, you don't mimic the standard (translated) alliterative verse line, with its three dutifully alliterating words and a space to indicate caesura. This is just a hint of what's to come, but it's already so different than even what Heaney was willing to do. The question then — and relate this back to the notion of visual structure if need be — how did you make such choices, and what balance did you try to strike between sound, sense, being "faithful" to the poem, and your own aesthetic procedure?

TM: That "Hwæt" did perplex me. There was a successful revival of [Jerome] Kern and [Oscar] Hammerstein's *Show Boat* in the West End [London] in 1971. Near the end of Act One, Captain Andy is concerned that although the house is filling up for that evening's performance, no "colored folks" are turning up when his cook, Queenie, shows him how to ballyhoo them. She shouts "Hey!" then vamps her spiel three or four more times. When I heard that, I thought, "That's it."

Embedded in there, too, was Thornton Wilder's transcription of some remarks made by Gertrude Stein at the University of Chicago on her American tour [1934] where she catches the audience's attention by shouting "Now listen!" Though that sounded a bit to class-roomy.

DH: To continue in this vein: The beginning of Fitt Five, which looks like a minimalist poem sculptured on the page; the description of Beowulf entering Heorot in Fitt Six, with single-word lines centered on the page; and finally, one of my favorite parts, your rendering of the fight with Grendel in Fitt 11, which reads in part:

> footstephandclawfiendreachmanbedquicktrick
> beastarmpainclampnewnotknownheartrunflesho
> feargetawaygonowrunrun
>
> never before had
> sinherd feared anything so.
>
> ("or cringed crushed . . .
>
> or my days' end . . ."
>
> Beowulf stoop up straight,
> beast in his grip,
> his knuckles popped.
> Ent bent on escape
>
> runwideflatopenswampholessafebadfingerman
> squeezeletgowantnotcomesadgobadhallrunrun

Here the reader is confronted with the words themselves running together, as if in panic, in much the same way that the original passage seems in such a rush to tell the story of the battle that bodies become confused, as in, for example, lines 748–50: "he quickly grabbed / with ill intent / and leaned on [Grendel's? his own?] arm," etc., wherein it's often difficult to tell with whom an action originates and who is being acted upon. This seems like a particularly provocative and brilliant solution to the translation problems presented by the passage.

Taken all together, this approach both brings to light a troubling assumption of most Old English verse translations, and proposes an interesting alternative. The assumption is that we can, and should want to, approximate a verse form that is based on oral transmission (and possibly aural composition). Your approach acknowledges that we don't have the cultural tools (or need) to do that anymore, as poets and listeners (readers) of poems. Instead, your text suggests that poems are now composed on the page, *as texts*, and challenges the reader in all the ways that twentieth-century long-form poetry can, from Pound's *Cantos* on down. So I'd really like to hear you say more about that, both in the context of typical translations of older texts, and the adventurous approaches put forward by Modernism, etc.

TM: The other two legs of my three-legged translation stool, besides Pound, were Zukofsky's Catullus[10] and Joyce's *Finnegan's Wake*.

Permission, as Robert Duncan might have it, for the inconsistent formalities all throughout my *Beowulf* was granted directly by Pound's "Propertius" where he runs the gamut from Victorian mediaeval to H.L. Menken wise-cracking. (Not to mention the variety of voices in his *Cantos*.) While Zukofsky's Catullus presented me with the idea of homophony dispensing with syntax, ironically even if the homophony wasn't present. And of course *Finnegan's Wake* provided the cloud-chamber for running words together. These were the tools to dismantle, then realign a text. Another influence was what would eventually become Christopher Logue's

---

[10] *Catullus* translated by Louis and Celia Zukofsky. See *Louis Zukofsky: Complete Short Poetry* (Baltimore: Johns Hopkins, 1991).

eight books of the Iliad, *War Music*,[11] its pace, and to some extent the look, in order to crack the mind-numbing, conventional, uniform stanza block after stanza block translation.

When I met Jonathan Williams in 1968 he was something of a kingpin in the International Concrete Poetry movement. However, it got much more attention in South America and Europe than in Britain or the U.S. Though, frankly, it struck me as dumb, literally and figuratively. Or too often clever and curious, risking cute. Also aligned with Jonathan, my interest in typography. Those two things were the big conscious push behind the page as a unit/recto-verso idea. You're right, although it wasn't a completely conscious strategy, these visual elements from Jonathan and Bunting's "end of the long poem" tipped me over from oral to visual as the answer, how to put across an old (epic) poem in 1972.

DH: What's been the impact of this translation work on your own poetic practice? You've published other translations — notably Sappho, and the *Tao Te Ching*. You've published a dozen-plus books of your own poetry. How has working with Old English at the outset of your career affected and perhaps shaped your other work in poetry?

TM: Hook, line, and sinker, at a young age, I swallowed Pound's dicta: translation is how you learn how to write a poem. It's only been since re-typing my *Beowulf* last summer that I've realized how profound an effect it's had on my work. For no other reason than the total textual immersion it and every other such project afforded me. All my translating has been of texts that drew themselves to me for one or another specific reason. My lack of linguistic expertise and cack-handed approach in each instance meant my focus was total, word for word. Skating on thin ice the whole time.

As I've said a couple times in this interview, the need to make the translation vital and various made me daring.

---

[11] Christopher Logue, *War Music: An Account of Books 1-4 and 16-19 of Homer's Iliad* (New York: Farrar, Straus, and Giroux, 1997).

DH: Finally, what kind of response did this translation receive around the time you did it? You mentioned Guy Davenport showing some interest, but eventually backing away. I would have thought that something of this nature would appeal to avant-garde poets and poetry movements as a way to build bridges to past poetries via contemporary innovations, and show what those innovations can accomplish in relation to older poetry. Sometimes I wonder if such movements get so attached to the idea of the "new" that they just don't want to deal with historical literature. Also, of course, there has always been a whiff of the "cultural purity," "desire for origins" aspect to philology and Old English in particular, though more recently, so-called "post-philology"[12] has opened things up again.

TM: Basil Bunting, my shade and mentor for this endeavor, to paraphrase Pound on H.D., found my *Beowulf* "fascinating if you can stand the quirkiness." That and Davenport's indifference — they were such towering figures for me at the time — led me to stick it in a drawer and go on to something else. Ann Lee and the Shakers, as it happened, a long poem that would include history.

Not being much of a self-promoter, and something of a "forest dweller," otherwise no one really saw it.

You know the elephant in the room is that *Beowulf* is really an odd work, an anomaly right from the start. Single extant manuscript, jumbled narrative, murky transition from oral to written, etc. etc. In the early 1970s no one was interested in that kind of textuality. Well, maybe in their own way, the French were. Certainly not Americans. From this, my present vantage, that was just what appealed to me. Subliminally. The liminality of the text. And now, as you suggest, there's a richer cultural context — and possible impact.

---

[12] See, for example, Michelle R. Warren, "Post-Philology," in *Postcolonial Moves: Medieval Through Modern*, eds. Patricia Clare Ingham and Michelle R. Warren (New York: Palgrave Macmillan, 2003), 19–46.

APPENDIX B

CRITICAL BIBLIOGRAPHY

BEOWULF EDITIONS

Beowulf: An Edition with Relevant Shorter Texts. Ed. Bruce Mitchell and Fred C. Robinson. Malden, MA: Blackwell, 2006.

Beowulf, A Student Edition. Ed. George Jack. New York: Oxford University Press, 1994.

Klaeber's Beowulf and the Fight at Finnsburg. 4th Edition. Ed. R.D. Fulk, Robert E. Bjork, and John D. Niles. Toronto: University of Toronto Press, 2008.

BEOWULF TRANSLATIONS

Alexander, Michael. *Beowulf: A Verse Translation*. Revised edition. New York: Penguin, 2003.

Chickering, Howell D. *Beowulf: A Dual-Language Edition*. New York: Anchor Book, 1977.

Greenfield, Stanley B. *A Readable Beowulf: The Old English Epic Newly Translated* (with an Introduction by Alain Renoir). Carbondale, IL: Southern Illinois University Press, 1982.

Liuzza, R. M. *Beowulf: A New Verse Translation*. Peterborough, Ontario: Broadview, 2000.

Morgan, Edwin. *Beowulf: A Verse Translation Into Modern English.* Berkeley: University of California Press, 1952.

Spicer, Jack. *Jack Spicer's Beowulf.* Parts I-II. Eds. David Hadbawnik and Sean Reynolds. CUNY Poetics Documents Initiative, Series 2.5 (Spring 2011).

ANGLO-SAXON CULTURE, OLD ENGLISH, AND *BEOWULF* SCHOLARSHIP

Baker, Peter S. *Introduction to Old English.* 2nd edition. Malden, MA: Blackwell, 2007.

Baker, Peter S., Editor. *Beowulf: Basic Readings.* New York: Garland, 1995.

Bjork, Robert E. and John D. Niles, eds. *A Beowulf Handbook.* Lincoln, NE: University of Nebraska Press, 1997.

Bonjour, Adrien. *The Digressions in "Beowulf."* Oxford, UK: Blackwell, 1950.

Brodeur, Arthur Gilchrist. *The Art of Beowulf.* Berkeley, CA: University of California Press, 1959.

Calder, Daniel G. Ed. *Old English Poetry: Essays On Style.* Berkeley, CA: University of California Press, 1979.

Earl, James W. *Thinking About Beowulf.* Stanford, CA: Stanford University Press, 1994.

Greenfield, Stanley B. and Calder, Daniel G. *A New Critical History of Old English Literature* (with a Survey of the Anglo-Latin background by Michael Lapidge). New York: New York University Press, 1986.

Hill, John M. *The Cultural World in Beowulf.* Toronto, Ontario: University of Toronto Press, 1995.

Kiernan, Kevin. *Beowulf and the Beowulf Manuscript*. New Brunswick, NJ: Rutgers University Press, 1981.

Leake, Jane Acomb. *The Geats of* Beowulf: *A Study in the Geographical Mythology of the Middle Ages*. Madison, WI: University of Wisconsin Press, 1967.

Magennis, Hugh. *Translating* Beowulf: *Modern Versions in English Verse*. Cambridge, UK: D.S. Brewer, 2011.

Mitchell, Bruce, and Robinson, Fred C. *A Guide to Old English*. 7th edition. Malden, MA: Blackwell, 1964.

Momma, Haruko. *The Composition of Old English Poetry*. Cambridge, UK: Cambridge University Press, 1997.

Nicholson, Lewis E. *An Anthology of "Beowulf" Criticism*. Notre Dame, IN: University of Notre Dame Press, 1963.

Overing, Gillian, and Marijane Osborn. *Landscape of Desire: Partial Stories of the Scandinavian World*. Minneapolis, MN: University of Minnesota Press, 2004.

The Postmodern Beowulf: A Critical Casebook. Ed. Eileen A. Joy and Mary K. Ramsay. Morgantown, WV: West Virginia University Press, 2006.

Robinson, Fred C. *Beowulf and the Appositive Style*. Knoxville, TN: University of Tennessee Press, 1985.

Russom, Geoffrey. *Beowulf and Old Germanic Metre*. New York: Cambridge University Press, 1998.

Tolkien, J.R.R. *"Beowulf: The Monsters and the Critics*. In *The Monsters and the Critics and Other Essays*. Boston, MA: Houghton Mifflin, 1984.

TWENTIETH-CENTURY POETRY

Bunting, Basil. *Briggflatts*. Fulcrum: 1966 (reprint Bloodaxe, 2009).

Duncan, Robert. *The Opening of the Field*. New York: New Directions, 1973.

Olson, Charles. *Collected Prose*. Ed. Donald Marriam Allen and Brian Friedlander. Berkeley, CA: University of California Press, 1997.

———. *The Maximus Poems*. Ed. George F. Butterick. Berkeley, CA: University of California Press, 1983.

Pound, Ezra. *The Cantos of Ezra Pound*. New York: New Directions, 1996.

———. *Personæ: The Shorter Poems*. Revised edition. New York: Directions, 1990.

Williams, William Carlos. *Patterson*. Revised edition. New York: New Directions, 1995.

Zukofsky, Louis. *"A"*. New York: New Directions, 2011.

———. *Prepositions: The Collected Critical Essays of Louis Zukofsky*. Expanded Edition. Berkeley, CA: University of California Press, 1981.

TWENTIETH-CENTURY POETRY CRITICISM

Blau DePlessis, Rachel, and Peter Quartermain, eds. *The Objectivist Nexus: Essays in Cultural Poetics*. Tuscaloosa, AL: University of Alabama Press, 1999.

Davidson, Michael. *Ghostlier Demarcations: Modern Poetry and the Material World*. Berkeley, CA: University of California Press, 1997.

Jones, Chris. *Strange Likeness: The Use of Old English in Twentieth-Century Poetry*. New York: Oxford University Press, 2006.

Nicholls, Peter. *George Oppen and the Fate of Modernism*. Oxford, UK: Oxford University Press, 2007.

Nichols, Miriam. *Radical Affections: Essays on the Poetics of Outside*. Tuscaloosa, AL: University of Alabama Press, 2010.

APPENDIX C

GLOSSARY OF NAMES AND NOTES

Note from Thomas Meyer: my Glossary follows Fr. Klaeber's derivations as given in his section on "Proper Names," *Beowulf and the Fight at Finnsburg*, 3rd edition. In a few instances I have hazarded guesses of my own. The order is alphabetical. *Italics* indicate a cross reference.

A
ABEL: Adam's son, *Cain*'s brother

AESCHERE: (Ash Spear) *Hrothgar*'s beloved warrior, counselor & companion

AESIR: (Gods) a race of Norse gods who wept when the world ended

AETHELBERHT: (Bright noble) king of East Anglia, suitor of *Offa*'s daughter

ANGLELAND: land of the *Angles*

ANGLES: a German tribe that settled in Britain & formed 3 kingdoms, East Anglia, *Mercia* & Northhumbria

B
BALDR: fairest of all Norse gods, one of the *Aesir*, whose death by arrow heralded earth's ruin & gods' dusk

BARDS: seafaring tribe, perhaps the Lombards, that lived for awhile on the south coast of the Baltic

BEANSTAN: (Shark) *Breca*'s father

BEEWOLF: hero of "The Bear's Son," rightfully confused with *Beowulf* the Geat

BEOWULF: the Dane (Barley Sheaf) *Scyld*'s son, early king of the *Danes*

BEOWULF the Geat: (Bee Wolf) noble king of the *Geats* whose story is worth the telling

BEOWULF: an Old English epic called after its hero, *Beowulf* the Geat, of which Fr. Klaeber has said:

"The reader of the poem very soon perceives that the progress of the narrative is frequently impeded. Looseness is, in fact, one of its marked peculiarities. Digression & episodes, general reflections in the form of speeches, an abundance of moralizing passages interrupt the story. There occur obvious gaps in the narrative. Furthermore, different parts of the story are sometimes told in different places, or substantially the same incident is related several times from different points of view."

BEOWULF'S BARROW: the mound built where Beowulf the Geat's pyre burned, a landmark

BRECA: (Storm) *Bronding*'s chief & Beowulf's swimming partner

BRONDINGS: (Ship's Prow) tribe of seafarers

BRONSINGS: (Fire Dwarfs) band of dwarfs who fashioned the ring or torc that *Hama* stole from *Eormenric* which originally belonged to one the *Aesir*, the goddess Freyja

C

CAIN: Adam's son, *Abel*'s brother & murderer who fostered an evil brood

CHARLEMAGNE: Carolingian king, *Thryth*'s cousin

D

DAEGHREFN: (Day Raven) Frankish warrior who never returned from war with Geats to bring his king the gem off *Hygelac*'s breast:

Beowulf's bare hands squeezed the last beat out of his heart. The Geat's grip left the Frank's frame a heap of crushed bone. Thus, through revenge, Beowulf evened the debt he owed Hygelac, paid for the land he'd leave his sons.

DANES: tribe that lived in the northern kingdom of *Denmark*

DENMARK: home of the *Danes*

E

EADGILS: (Wealth's Hostage) *Ohthere*'s son who, with his brother *Eanmund*, crossed the sealake to seek refuge with *Heardred*:

Their uncle, *Onela*, seized the *Scylfings*' throne from their father & they had to flee Sweden for fear of their lives. Hygelac's son welcomed them but in return set the seal upon his own fate. His open arms were rewarded with sword's edge when Onela attacked the Geats. Both Eanmund & Heardred fell in that fight. However, Eadgils escaped. When that invading army withdrew they left Beowulf in command. Thus that noble warrior came to the throne he'd once refused. Years later the old Geat, heeding the vengeance due for Heardred's death, sent armies across the great lake to aid Eadgils' attacks upon his uncle, Onela. With Geats' help his forces grew in might until he was able to claim his own rightful vengeance by taking his uncle's life.

EANMUND: (Delivering Hand) *Eadgil*'s brother

EAGLE NESS: promontory in *Geats*' Land near where *Beowulf*'s last stand took place

ECGLAF: (Sword Remnant) Danish warrior, *Unferth*'s father

ECGTHEOW: (Sword Servant) *Beowulf*'s father

ECGWELA: (Sword Wealth) Danish patriarch

EIDER: river in *Angles*' former lands which forms the boundary between Schleswig & Holstein

EOFOR: (Boar) Geat who slayed *Ongentheow* at *Ravenswood*

EOMER: (Renowned Horse) Angle prince, *Offa*'s son

EORMENRIC: (Great Power) king of East Goths who at one time possessed the *Bronsings*' torc

F

FINN: king of the East *Frisians*

FINNS: tribe living in northern Norway

FITELA: (Gray Wolf) *Sigemund*'s nephew & son

Note: errata, in OVERSEA, the tale told there of Fitela & Sigemund confuses their relationship making uncle nephew & nephew uncle.

FOLCWADA: (People's Protection) *Finn's* father

FREAWARU: (Watchful of the Lord) *Hrothgar's* daughter

FRISIA: territory in Friesland west of the Zuider Zee

FRISIAN: tribe that lived in Friesland or *Frisia*

FRODA: (Wise) *Ingeld's* father, a *Bard* chief

G
GARMUND: (Spear Band) king of Mercia, Offa's father:

Although he lived to a ripe old age & was loved by his people, Garmund had no children except for a son, *Offa*, whom he considered unfit as his heir. The boy had been both dumb & blind from birth, & when he gained his sight at the age of 7, he still remained silent, uttering no human word. This caused Garmund great sorrow & troubled his people no end. The old king, certain his death was not long off, did not know whom to appoint as his successor & heir. An evil Mercian chief, seeing Garmund grow old without hope of begetting another son, plagued the old man day after day, asking him whom he'd appointed as heir. Then the wicked chief gathered his supporters & began to hold public debates to discuss this urgent matter & to select Gamund's successor. Dumb Offa attended these meetings & listened to every word spoken at them. It was at one of these debates that the boy thought a fool uttered his first words.

GEATS: tribe that lived in southern Sweden

GIFTHAS: tribe that once lived at the mouth of the Wisla in Poland & later moved to the lower Danube

GOD: the hand & wisdom that guides the hearts of true warriors & noble kings

GRENDEL: (Grinder) one of the evil brood fostered by *Cain*

GUNLAF: (War Remnant) Danish warrior

H

HALGA: (Holy) Danish prince, *Hrothgar*'s younger brother

> *Note*: errata, in OVERSEA, Halga is wrongly called Helga & identified as a daughter of Hrothgar.

HAMA: (Homeland) outlawed or exiled Goth, companion of Wudga & hero of a cycle of tales

HARETH: (Spoils of War) *Hygd*'s father

HEALFDENE: (Half Dane) Danish king, *Hrothgar*'s father

HEARDRED: (Fixed) *Hygelac*'s son, king of Geats slain by *Onela*

HEATHOLAF: (War Remnant) *Wyfing* warrior slain by *Ecgtheow*

HEATHORAEMAS: race that lived in southern Norway

HELMINGS: (Principle) *Wealhtheow*'s family

HEMMING: (Shoe) some kin of *Offa* & his son *Eomer*

HENGEST: (Horse) chief of the Danes under *Healfdene*

HEOROGAR: (Army Spear) Danish king, *Hrothgar*'s older brother

HEOROT: (Hart) the goldhall *Hrothgar* built

HEREBALD: (Battle Brave) prince of Geats, *Hrethel*'s oldest son

HEREMOND: (War Mind) prehistoric king of Danes who ruled long before *Scyld*

HETWARE: (Helmet People) tribe of *Franks* that lived on the lower Rhine

HILDEBURH: (Battle Hill) *Finn*'s wife

HNAEF: (Bowed Down) chief of Danes under *Healfdene*

HOC: (Kid) *Hildeburgh* & *Hnaef*'s father

HOTHCYN: (War Type) prince of Geats, *Hrethel*'s second son

HROTHR: blind god, one of the *Aesir*, who was tricked by Loki into shooting *Baldr* with a mistletoe arrow

HREOSNA HILL: hill in Geats' land

HRETHEL: (Quick Victory) king of the Geats, *Hygelac*'s father, *Beowulf*'s grandfather

HRETHRIC: (Victory Rich) *Hrothgar*'s son

HROTHGAR: (Victory Spear) Danes' king

HROTHULF: (Victory Wolf) *Halga*'s son, *Hrothgar*'s nephew

HRUNTING: (Thrust) *Unferth*'s sword

HUNAFING: (Left Thigh) warrior in *Hengest*'s band

HYGD: (Thought) *Hygelac*'s wife

HYGELAC: (Battle Gift) king of Geats who lost his life in *Frisia*:

The *Hetware*'s blades beat him down, their swords slaked their thirst with his blood. Yet Beowulf, after killing Daegnhrefn in revenge for Hygelac's death, got away safely. As he ran for the sea, he left in his path few Hetware who would ever see their hall & homes again or sing of that battle. At land's edge he jumped into the flood, clutching 30 mailshirts & swam the vast water home to Geats.

Upon return, Hygd offered him her dead husband's kingdom, throne & hoard. She wasn't sure her son, Heardred, could protect Geats' land from foreign invasions. But nothing could persuade Beowulf to take what rightfully belonged to Hygelac's heir. However, with his advice & goodwill, friendship & respect, he supported the young king until he was old enough to rule Geats on his own.

I

INGELD: (Ing's Payment) *Froda*'s son, *Bard* prince

INGWINE: (Ing's Friends) the Danes

J

JUTES: Frisian tribe, King *Finn*'s people

K

KRAKEN LAKE: (Sea Monster Lake) name for the lake on the bottom of which *Grendel* & his mother lived

M

MERCIA: one of the 3 *Angle* kingdoms, its king *Offa*

MEROVINGIAN: king of the *Franks*

MIDGARTH: (Middle Enclosure) central part of the universe enclosed by seas, where men dwell, & sometimes called Middle Earth

MONSTER MERE: (Monster's Water) *Grendel's* lake

N

NAEGLING: (Studded) *Beowulf's* sword

O

OFFA: (Wolf) king of *Mercia*, *Garmund's* son

As a boy he was tall, sturdy & handsome but could neither see nor speak. At 7 years his eyes cleared & he saw, but his tongue stayed thick, his lips mute. His father considered him unfit as heir to Mercia's throne & was forced by an evil chief with royal aspirations to hold a series of debates at which a successor would be appointed. Offa's keen ears took in every word said at these meetings. When he heard how his father was abused & that he himself was despised & blamed for all his kingdom's misfortune, the boy's heart welled with tears that flooded his eyes, streaming down his face & wetting his lips.

He prayed to God for comfort, guidance, wisdom & salvation. The Lord to whom all things lie naked & open heard this dumb plea & unsealed the boy's lips with clear, kingly words:

> Why do you abuse my father,
> & blame me for your misfortunes?
> He's been a good king
> & I'm his rightful heir so
> why do you want a wicked man,
> stained with crime, to sit on your throne?

Those gathered there were speechless. Garmund then asked his son why, if he could speak so clearly, had he not done so before:

> Because, Father, there was no need to until now, your protection satisfied me but now I see you need my aid if we're to keep our kingdom pure, safe from evil.

Thus Offa proved himself a worthy heir & when Garmund died, succeeded his father as a good, noble Mercian king taking as his queen a woman called *Thryth*.

OHTHERE: (Pursuing Army) *Ogentheow*'s son who became the Swedes' king when his father fell at *Ravenswood*, & was succeeded by his brother *Onela*

ONELA: *Ogentheow*'s son & *Ohthere*'s brother, Swedish king who lost his life in a battle fought with his nephew, *Eadgils*

ONGENTHEOW: (Adverse Servant) king of Sweden who sent his sons, *Onela* & *Ohthere*, across the sealake to raid Geats' land:

Most of their attacks were made in the shadow of Hreosna Hill. At Ravenswood that king struck down Hothcyn & in return Eofor took revenge by slaying Ongentheow. Some say all that happened that day at Ravenswood had been laid out by fate months before when the old Scylding suffered a boarwound while hunting in that wood.

OSLAF: (God's Heritage) Danish warrior

R

RAVENSWOOD: forest in *Sweden* where *Geats* made their first attack upon *Scylfings*:

Outraged by that sudden outbreak of war on his own soil, the terrible old king struck down the seafarers' captain. He then rescued his wife, Onela & Othere's mother, an old woman stripped of her gold, & pursued Hothcyn's army as it retreated into the wood, lost & confused without its leader. When night fell Ongentheow's men camped at the edge of Ravenswood. The grayhaired warchief chanted over the fire:

> The Geats our blades don't bite
> will swing from trees, meat for
> this dark woods' black ravens.
>
> Our gods prepare their crows a
> bloody breakfast of morning gore.

Hygelac's horn broke the air & dawn's firstlight lifted the hearts of grieving warriors deep inside Ravenswood. Their king & his men had found their trail & followed them there. Far & wide along bloodshed's path, the rescuing army beheld slaughter's pitch: dead Swedes & Geats littered the trail.

Fast thinking Ongentheow, alarmed by this new development, hurried his men onto higher ground, up to a more sheltered spot. He was well acquainted with Hygelac's skillful tactics & wasn't sure his army could hold back the seafarers or guard his hoard & protect his tribe's women & children against Geats' onslaught. The old man's troops stood ready behind earthwalls. Hygelac's banners overran Swedes. Hrethel's Geats swarmed their camp. Ongentheow found himself face to face with Wulf & Eofor, Wonred's sons. Wulf lunged. The rage in his stroke broke a blood vessel on his scalp. The old Scylfing turned, returned a fiercer stroke that left Wulf wounded. His helmet split. He fell to the ground, covered in blood from a deep head gash, yet still among the living.

Eofor saw his brother cringe & swung his blade wide. His entmade sword cracked Ongentheow's trollmade helmet, halving his skull. The Scylfings' king lay dead in the dirt. In no time at all, men bound Wulf's wounds & carried him away. The field was now clear & the Geats slaughter's masters. Eofor undid Ongentheow's iron byrne, pulled off his helmet, took away his sword. These he brought to Hygelac who thanked the warrior & promised to reward him well for those spoils of war.

Geats then carried Ongentheow's body back down to Ravenswood & laid it aloft a pile of boughs & let wild birds & beasts tear his flesh from his bones. They made a crow from wood smeared with the old Scylfing's blood & sent it back to the Swedes.

When he got home, Hrethel's son gave Wulf & Eofor gold as reward for war's storm. The glory their strokes earned them brought them great riches: land & linked rings worth 100,000 sceattas. No man on Midgarth questioned the favors those brothers won. Eofor also received Hygelac's only daughter to wive & bless his hearth with friendship's pledge of honor.

S

SCANDINAVIA: northern kingdoms of *Denmark, Sweden &
Norway*

SCYLD SCEFING: (Sheaf Shield) early Danish king

SCYLDINGS: (Children of Scyld) the *Danes*

SCYLFINGS: (Children of Crags) the *Swedes*

SEAGEATS: the *Geats*

SIGEMUND: (Victory Hand) *Wael*'s son, uncle & father of
Fitela

SWEDES: northern tribe that lived northwest of Lake Väner &
Vätter

SWEDEN: kingdom of the *Swedes*

SWERTING: (Black) *Hygelac*'s maternal uncle

T

THYTH: (Strength) *Offa*'s wife, cousin of *Charlemagne*

TROLL KILLER: early, pagan god of *Danes*

U

UNFERTH: (Unpeaceful) warrior & member of *Hrothgar*'s
court

V

VENDELS: tribe that lived in Uppland, *Sweden* or in Vendill, northern Juteland.

W

WAEGMUNDINGS: (Children of the Wave's Grasp) family of *Weohstan, Wiglaf* & *Beowulf*

WAELS: the *Geats*

WEALHTHEOW: (Foreign or Celtic Hostage) *Hrothgar*'s wife, queen of *Danes*

WEDERS: (Weatherers) the *Geats*

WEDERLAND: *Geats'* land

WELAND: (Craft) legendary ironsmith

WEOHSTAN: (Battle Rock) *Wiglaf*'s father, a *Waegmunding* who fought for *Swedes:*

In battle he slew Eanmund. Onela rewarded him with the dead warrior's sword & wargear. An uncle gave gifts to his nephew's murderer. But when Eanmund's brother, Eadgils, seized the throne, Weohstan had to flee back to Geats' land. He brought with him the entmade blade, a bright helmet & gleaming ringbyrne.

Weaostan kept those treasures many years & when his son, Wiglaf, had proven himself worthy of them, they passed into that young hero's hands. The father presented his son with that wargear before he died. They were an honor not an inheritance.

WHALE NESS: headland on the coast of *Geats'* land, site of *Beowulf's Barrow*

WIGLAF: (War Heritage) *Beowulf's* kinsman, a *Waegmunding*

WULF: (Wolf) *Eofor's* brother, a *Geat* who fought at *Ravenswood*

WULFGAR: (Wolf Spear) *Vendel* chief, official at *Heorot*

WYLFINGS: (Children of the Wolf) tribe that lived south of the Baltic

Y

YRMENLAF: (Great Heritage) *Aeschere's* brother, a *Dane*

YRSE: (Anger) *Hrothgar's* sister, *Onela's* wife

punctum books is an open-access and print-on-demand independent publisher dedicated to radically creative modes of intellectual inquiry and writing across a whimsical para-humanities assemblage. We specialize in neo-traditional and non-conventional scholarly work that productively twists and/or ignores academic norms, with an emphasis on books that fall length-wise between the article and the monograph—id est, novellas, in one sense or another. We also take in strays. This is a space for the imp-orphans of your thought and pen, an ale-serving church for little vagabonds.

http://punctumbooks.com